AMERICAN LITERACY

AMERICAN LITERACY

Fifty Books
That Define
Our Culture
and Ourselves

J. NORTH CONWAY

WILLIAM MORROW AND COMPANY, INC.

NEW YORK

Library of Congress Cataloging-in-Publication Data

Conway, J. North (Jack North)
    American literacy: fifty books that define our culture and ourselves
    / by J. North Conway.
        p.   cm.
    Includes index.
    ISBN 0-688-11963-8
    1. Books and reading — United States.   2. Authors and readers —
United States.   3. Literature and society — United States.
4. United States — Civilization.   I. Title.
    Z1002.2.C66   1993
    028'.9'0973 — dc20   93-2654
                                                                    CIP

Printed in the United States of America

1   2   3   4   5   6   7   8   9   10

First Edition

BOOK DESIGN BY LISA STOKES

Acknowledgments

This book is dedicated to my lovely wife, Julia, and my son, Nate, who have given me more love and joy than anyone should expect.

I could not have completed this book without the expert research of Ruth Sullivan and the vast resources of Bristol Community College's Learning Resource Center.

I wish to thank my agent, Jim Trupin, and my editors, Randy Ladenheim-Gil, Tom Darling, and Joan Marlow for their help, and I would also like to thank Janice Richards for her exceptional services.

Special thanks are extended to the *Taunton Daily Gazette*, where portions of this book originally appeared, and the very kind and helpful people at the Boston Public Library, the Taunton Public Library, and the Library of Congress. I wish to thank Bill and Barbara Wagner for their help and support (so it goes); Frank and Lorraine McNally for showing me around Philadelphia, "the Cradle of Liberty," where many of the words in this book originated; and Neva Flaherty and Read Kingsbury, for the use of their exquisite porch at the Bellevue House on Block Island, where much of this book was edited. Thank you one and all.

Contents

Introduction
Why Books Make a Difference

Since this country's earliest beginnings, books and writers have played an important role in shaping the world we live in. We have seen our own hopes, dreams, and ideals reflected in their words. This book is a sampling of a mere fifty books and writers that have helped shape America. This is by no means all of them.

In making my selections, I have drawn on several existing sources, as well as applying my own criteria. My primary source was the results of a survey conducted by the Port Washington, New York, Public Library on the occasion of its hundredth anniversary, held in 1992. The survey asked many distinguished Americans, among them former president Jimmy Carter, Supreme Court justice Sandra Day O'Connor, economist and author John Kenneth Galbraith, and columnist George Will, to submit a list of books that have "profoundly affected the thoughts and actions of humankind." I have included many of the American-authored books that appeared in this noteworthy survey.

According to Michael D'Innocenzo, professor of history at Hofstra University, who was deeply involved in the Port Washington survey, "Great books help to elevate the human spirit by addressing issues that transcend a particular time or place."

The books I have chosen were not selected because they were best-sellers, although many of them were. They were chosen because of the impact they had on American society and laws.

My father convinced me that "the pen is mightier than the sword."

"And besides, you don't have to wear a scabbard," he would joke.

For many years, he was the editor and publisher of a small weekly newspaper on the East Side of Providence, Rhode Island, near Brown University, where he went to school. Because of him, books, newspapers, and magazines have been a big part of my life.

Some people would like you to believe that movies and television have rendered reading books obsolete, but a recent Gallup Poll suggests that reading is on the rise. According to the poll, 45 percent of adults polled said they planned to read more in the 1990s. That's good news for America.

More than any other medium, books have helped shape the world we live in. Books mean the world to some people. Literally.

America is not named after the man who discovered it, but after Amerigo Vespucci, the man who wrote about it. Had it not been for Vespucci and the book *Cosmographiae Introductio*, published in 1507, we would all be pledging allegiance to the United States of Columbia.

The written word has played a significant role in determining who and what we are politically from Thomas Paine's

"American Crisis Papers," which kept the American Revolution going through its darkest days, to this country's most famous political document, The Declaration of Independence, written by Thomas Jefferson.

The impact of American books has been felt around the world, spanning generations. Henry David Thoreau's "Civil Disobedience" was the theoretical foundation of Gandhi's movement in India and Martin Luther King, Jr.'s civil-rights movement in America.

Many books have helped create the laws that govern the way we live. Samuel Hopkins Adams's book *The Great American Fraud*, published in 1906, led to the passage of the Pure Food and Drug Act. Upton Sinclair's *The Jungle* exposed the Chicago meat-packing industry and led to legislation requiring the inspection of beef. Jessica Mitford's book *The American Way of Death*, published in 1963, exposed abuses in the funeral industry and led to legislation to protect consumers from this woeful fraud. There are many more books upon which we have built our laws.

Books have exposed the flaws in our society and helped correct them. Harriet Beecher Stowe's *Uncle Tom's Cabin* was called by President Lincoln the single most influential argument for enacting the Emancipation Proclamation. Rachel Carson's book *The Silent Spring*, published in 1962, exposed the dangers of pollution for the first time to a mass audience and spawned a whole generation of environmental activism. And Michael Harrington's *The Other America*, also published in 1962, exposed the issue of deep-rooted poverty in America and served as the impetus for President Lyndon Johnson's war on poverty.

Even the things we take for granted have frequently come about because of books. Noah Webster's *Spelling Book*, published in 1783, standardized the spelling of the American language for the first time. Fannie Farmer's *The Boston Cooking-School Cook Book*, published in 1896, first introduced standard cooking measurements into American society. And Dr. Benjamin Spock's *The Common Sense Book of Baby and Child Care*, published in 1946, became the Bible for child rearing in this country. The list of books that helped shape this country goes on and on.

As Americans, we need to discuss the issues that confront this great nation, not as a matter of politics, but as part of our collective American experience. There are many more books that need to be written, about issues that this country needs to resolve, which is why books play such an important part in our lives. The changes in our society will *not* come from television or from movies, but from the written word.

In his 1962 Nobel Prize acceptance speech, John Steinbeck said, "The ancient commission of the writer has not changed. He is charged with exposing our many grievous faults and failures, with dredging up to light our dark and dangerous dreams for the purpose of improvement."

The following is a sampling of books and writers that kept faith with what Steinbeck called "the ancient commission."

"Don't join the book burners. Don't think you are going to conceal faults by concealing the evidence that they ever existed. Don't be afraid to go in your library and read every book."

DWIGHT D. EISENHOWER

1 Amerigo Vespucci (1454–1512)
Cosmographiae Introductio, 1507

"To make discovery, not to make a profit."

*A*merica is not named after Christopher Columbus, who discovered it, but after Amerigo Vespucci, the man who wrote about it. Had it not been for Vespucci and the book *Cosmographiae Introductio*, published in 1507 by an obscure French clergyman named Martin Waldseemüller, we would be pledging allegiance to the United States of Columbia.

Vespucci was born into a wealthy family in Florence, Italy, in 1454. He studied astronomy, geography, and navigation, and ultimately went into the merchant-banking business. Lured by adventure and, in his own words, the desire to ". . . make discovery, not to make a profit," Vespucci set sail for the New World.

There is no doubt that Vespucci made several trips to the New World, but exactly *when* he made his first voyage has been the basis of centuries of scholarly debate. Vespucci claimed he made his first trip in 1497, a full year before Columbus discovered what is now the continent of South America. In 1492, Columbus landed in Cuba, not realizing the full extent of the

North American continent. Most historical scholars agree that Vespucci's maiden voyage to the New World was made in 1499, not 1497, as he claimed. Whether he was the first to discover the South American continent or not didn't matter to the people who read his accounts of the New World.

In his letters to his Florentine benefactors, Vespucci wrote vividly of the New World paradise he claimed to have discovered.

"This land is very delightful, and covered with an infinite number of green trees and very big ones that never lose their foliage," he wrote, ". . . throughout the year [they] yield the sweetest aromatic perfumes and produce an infinite number of fruits, grateful to the taste and healthful for the body . . . ."

According to Vespucci, the New World was teaming with exotic wildlife: ". . . [the] multitude of wild animals, the abundance of pumas, of panthers, of wild cats . . . of so many wolves, red deer, monkeys . . . and many large snakes . . . so many species could not have entered Noah's ark.

". . . what shall I say of the quantity of birds and their plumage, and their songs, and of such variety and beauty . . ."

Vespucci's descriptions of the New World and its inhabitants were sexy and lurid. He wrote that both the men and women went naked and engaged in uninhibited sex.

"Their marriages are not with one woman but with as many as they like . . . when their children . . . the girls, reach the age of puberty, the first man to corrupt them must be their nearest relative.

". . . those that they capture, they take home as slaves, and if women, they sleep with them. . . ."

It was sensational writing compared to the dull accounts of the New World that Columbus prepared for Queen Isabella's court.

Vespucci described the natives as cannibals who cut up and

ate their dead enemies. ". . . one of their men confessed to me that he had eaten the flesh of more than 200 bodies. . . ."

Vespucci's letters about the exotic new lands and the people who inhabited them were widely circulated. The European public clamored after news about the New World. For many years, news about the discoveries was limited to the courts of kings.

In 1506, Vespucci's letters were collected and published in Florence. An illustrated pamphlet called *The Four Voyages of Amerigo Vespucci* became the most popular publication in Europe. There were some forty editions in print, with translations in Italian, French, German, and Latin. During the twenty-five years following the discovery of the New World, publications of Vespucci's adventures surpassed those of Columbus three times over.

In 1507, an obscure French clergyman named Martin Waldseemüller published a small 103-page book on world geography called *Cosmographiae Introductio*. Although Waldseemüller intended it as a scholarly publication, he included the text of the Vespucci pamphlet. In the introduction, Waldseemüller proposed that the new world be named after Vespucci.

". . . a fourth part (of the world) has been discovered by Amerigo Vespucci. Inasmuch as both Europe and Asia received their name from women, I see no reason why we should not call it Amerige or America, after its discoverer."

Waldseemüller included a map of the world in the book with the word "America" imprinted across the newly discovered continent.

Cosmographiae Introductio became an instant best-seller. Originally published in April 1507, it sold out, and a second edition was published in August. No one, including Martin Waldseemüller, understood the far-reaching impact the book would have. Even when Waldseemüller was convinced that Vespucci's claims were false, it was too late. The maps of "America" as it appeared in Waldseemüller's book had been distributed throughout Europe. In later editions, Waldseemüller took the name off the map, but by then the public at large found the name so appealing that it was adopted by public acclaim. By 1538, all of Europe began calling both continents of the New World "America."

Vespucci had nothing to do with promoting the idea that the New World be named after him. He was content to live out his years in Florence, where he died in 1512, unaware that half the world would bear his name.

2 Stephen Day (c.1594–1668)
The Bay Psalm Book, 1640

*"Conscience, rather than elegance, fidelity,
rather than poetry."*

THE TIMES: The Colonial population of America was
nearly twenty-eight thousand. The first federation of New
England colonies, representing Massachusetts Bay, Plymouth,
New Haven, and Connecticut, was formed. The first textile
mill and the first successful ironworks were established in Massachusetts. Roger Williams, the founder of Rhode Island, com-
piled the first Indian-language dictionary, called *A Key into the
Language of America*, which was published in England.

Stephen Day, a nearly illiterate locksmith from Cambridge,
Massachusetts, printed the first full-length book in North
America and unlocked the door to America's preeminence in
publishing.

The Bay Psalm Book, as it has become known, was published
in 1640 in Cambridge. *The Whole Booke of Psalms Faithfully
Translated into English Metre* (the official title of the book) was
prepared and published by a committee of Puritan ministers,
including Richard Mather, Thomas Welde, and John Eliot.

Massachusetts Bay Puritan ministers like Mather wanted their own psalm book to distinguish themselves from their Pilgrim neighbors living in the Plymouth Bay Colony. They also wanted a psalm book that adhered more closely to the biblical texts.

According to Mather, his intent and that of his fellow ministers was to create a psalm book that was a work of "Conscience rather than elegance, fidelity, rather than poetry." No music was printed in *The Bay Psalm Book*. Members of each congregation were required to create their own music for the psalms. Although this ad hoc form of psalm singing was musically unsophisticated, it did give church members a means of singing God's praise.

Another practice was for the minister of the church to read the psalm aloud, line by line, so the congregation could follow along. This custom, known as "lining out," has remained in practice into the twentieth century, especially in the rural South, where literacy is sometimes a problem.

When Mather and the other ministers completed the new translations of the psalms, they were taken to Stephen Day for publication. Day came to America from London with Joseph Glover, a rector from Surrey, England. Glover had long dreamed of establishing his own printing press in the Colonies.

Glover hired Day as a workman and paid for his passage to America. Glover brought along with him a printing press and a quantity of paper and type. He had made no mention to the English authorities of his intention to begin a printing house in the Colonies. Instead, he listed his occupation as a clerk and Day's as a locksmith, which he had been in London. Glover hoped to avoid repercussions from the English authorities, who had no desire to see a freestanding printing press established in the New World.

Joseph Glover died on the voyage to America. His wife, Elizabeth, brought the printing press to Cambridge, Massachusetts, and took over the business of running it. Mrs. Glover bought a house in Market Square in Cambridge, where she provided Stephen Day with lodging at a nearby house on Crooked Lane.

Day managed the day-to-day operation of the press. In 1639, he turned out a broadside called *The Freeman's Oath*, and later that same year, he published a pamphlet called *An Almanack Calculated for New England*, written by William Pierce. These two documents are considered the first two documents printed in the Massachusetts Bay Colony. No copies of *The Freeman's Oath* or Pierce's *Almanack* exist today.

Day undertook the printing of *The Bay Psalm Book* in July 1640. The book measured five-and-one-half inches by seven inches, and it contained 148 pages. Seventeen hundred copies of it were printed and sold for twenty pence each. According to Day's records, a profit of approximately eighty pounds was made from its sale.

By today's publishing standards, the book was a designer's nightmare and a publisher's worst dream. No spacing was provided between the various psalms. Sometimes the title of a psalm appeared at the end of one page, with the text appearing on the following page. Different typefaces and type sizes were used throughout the book, including some Greek and Hebrew characters. Ornamental imprints were placed randomly throughout the book in an effort to decorate the pages. The punctuation in the text was deplorable, with periods left out and commas inserted where they didn't belong. Often, one-syllable words were hyphenated, while other words that should have been divided at the end of a verse remained intact. Even the word "psalm" was misspelled on alternating pages of the book. It appeared in the left-hand corner of the pages as "Psalm," while it was printed on the right hand corner of the page as "Psalme."

Most of these errors can be attributed to Day's limited knowledge of the English language and because type for the book had to be set entirely by hand, a painstaking process even for someone who *could* employ consistency in spelling, punctuation, etc. It must also be acknowledged that in Day's time rules to standardize the written language had not yet been codified.

According to the errata page in the book, the printer listed only seven errors overall. A quick scan of the book reveals nearly twenty times that many. It is noted in the book by Day that the "rest of the faults which have escaped through oversight you may amend as you find obvious. . . ."

In 1641, Elizabeth Glover married Henry Dunster, the first president of Harvard College (Harvard University). Dunster took over the management of the printing press and moved the printing operation into his home on the Harvard campus.

Elizabeth Dunster died in 1643. In 1654, Henry Dunster retired from Harvard and sold the press to the college. The simple handpress was the forerunner of the Harvard University Press, one of the oldest university-based publishing houses in the country. The establishment of this press in Cambridge, and the appearance of subsequent freestanding presses, gave the Massachusetts Bay Colony an advantage over other colonies that had to rely on presses owned and operated by Englishmen.

As a printer, Stephen Day made very little money and soon found himself in debt. He worked for Mrs. Glover, and later for Henry Dunster, until about 1649, when he resigned. He later went to work full time in the more lucrative locksmith profession.

Day went on to become a prosperous landowner in Cambridge and died there in 1668. His name does not appear on any of the publications printed by this first Cambridge press, not even on the famous *Bay Psalm Book*.

Only eleven of the original seventeen hundred copies of the book remain in existence today. Only five of these remaining copies are complete. It is considered one of the rarest books in the country and a coveted prize for book collectors. In 1947, a copy of the book sold for an estimated $151,000 in a New York City auction.

All but one of the existing copies of the book remain in America, in the possession of public facilities, including the John Carter Brown Library in Providence, Rhode Island, the Yale University Library, and the Harvard University Library.

Benjamin Franklin (1706–90)
Experiments and Observations on Electricity, Made at Philadelphia in America, 1751–54

3

> *"He snatched the lightning from the sky and the scepter from the tyrant."*

THE TIMES: The Colonial population was 1.2 million. Benjamin Franklin published America's first political cartoon in the *Pennsylvania Gazette*. Captioned "Join or Die," the cartoon depicted a snake cut into eight sections, with the head representing Massachusetts and the other sections representing the remaining colonies. The first general hospital was founded in Philadelphia. A black man, Benjamin Banneker, built the first clock made in America.

Of all his accomplishments, it was Benjamin Franklin's shortest and least-read book that electrified the world!

It may come as a shock to learn that Franklin was not the first person to discover that lightning was electricity by conducting an experiment with a kite and a key. Still, Franklin practically single-handedly defined modern electrical science. Franklin's *Experiments and Observations on Electricity, Made at*

Philadelphia in America, published in England in 1751, was the most influential scientific book produced in Colonial America. Less than ninety pages long and based solely on a collection of private letters, the book became so popular among European scientists that ten editions were printed prior to the American Revolution, and it was translated into a dozen languages.

Franklin's experiments with electricity lasted a scant six years, approximately 1746 to 1752; the benefits derived from those experiments, however, have lasted centuries.

The contents of this slim volume revolutionized scientific thought in the field of electricity, defined the scientific terminology that is still used today, and secured Franklin a place in history as one of the first electrical scientists of his age.

His interest in electricity was piqued after a trip to Boston, where he witnessed a demonstration of the first Leyden jar. He was thirty-seven years old at the time. In 1745, in Leyden, Germany, Pieter van Musschenbroek invented a glass jar that could conduct electricity. This earliest of condensers was a glass bottle, covered with metal foil and filled with water or gunshot, in which a wire hook was placed. Electrical sparks could be produced in the jar by placing a conductor to both sides of the bottle.

Little was known about electricity during Franklin's age, and the Leyden jar was used mostly for entertainment. There are scores of tales from this period depicting how electricity was used to send brilliant flashes of colored lights across darkened rooms for the enjoyment of audiences. In some instances, it was used to electrocute live chickens and roast meat.

One story, of the amazing electrified monks, tells how Louis XV lined up seven hundred monks holding a wire. When the first monk touched an electrical conductor and the last monk touched a condenser, all 700 monks flew into the air.

Because of his scientific leanings, Franklin was intrigued

by what electricity was and how it worked. There were many scientific books written about the subject, most speculating on the composition of electricity, but there was very little true scientific experimentation and no practical application for this powerful energy source. Based on his thorough analysis of the Leyden jar, Franklin concluded correctly that the charge inside the jar was negative, while the charge outside was positive, both charges equally balancing the other. This was the most far-reaching discovery made in the field of electrical science. The terms coined by Franklin for these charges, positive and negative, plus and minus, are still used today.

Through further experiments, Franklin discovered that the shape of the Leyden jar had little to do with the current of electricity it was able to hold. Based on this discovery, Franklin developed and named the first electrical battery. He replaced the glass jar with a series of glass plates.

"Upon this we made what we called an electrical battery consisting of eleven panes of large sash-glass, armed with thin lead plates, pasted on each side. . . ." Franklin wrote. Franklin chose to call it a battery, after the military term, because of the powerful electric shock it produced.

Out of Franklin's electrical experiments came much of today's electrical-science terminology including the terms "charge" and "discharge," "condenser," "conductor," "electrical shock," and even "electrician."

During his experiments with electricity, Franklin confessed that no other subject "so totally engrossed my attention and my time. . . ."

The great myth surrounding Franklin's electricity experiments was that he discovered that lightning was electricity by flying a kite with a key attached to it during a thunderstorm. This is not completely true. Franklin did use a kite and key to show that lightning was electricity, but the experiment was conducted after the fact had already been proved. What Franklin did was propose an experiment that would determine the nature of lightning.

Franklin wrote in 1750, "To determine the question whether the clouds that contain lightning are electrified or no, I would propose an experiment . . . . On the top of some high tower or steeple, place a kind of sentry box, big enough to contain a man and an electrical stand. From the middle of the stand let an iron rod raise. . . ."

While Franklin was waiting to find a building or steeple high enough to conduct his experiment from in Philadelphia, his book *Experiments and Observations on Electricity, Made at Philadelphia in America* was published. The book was translated into French, and Jean-François D'Alibard, a French scientist, erected an iron rod forty feet into the air in an attempt to prove Franklin's theory. On May 10, 1752, a single bolt of lightning hit the apparatus, sending an electrical charge down the length of the iron rod. The true identity of lightning was confirmed.

Approximately six months after D'Alibard had proved the true nature of lightning, Franklin and his son flew a kite into a thunderstorm. A wire was attached to the top of the kite, and a metal key and strip of silk ribbon were tied at the end of the kite's string. The string became wet, and Franklin was able to snatch lightning from the sky and store it in a Leyden jar.

Franklin's account of his kite experiment was published fifteen years later by Joseph Priestley (1733–1804), the noted British theologian and chemist.

". . . having published his method of verifying his hypothesis concerning the sameness of electricity with the matter of lightning, [he] was waiting for the erection of a spire in Philadelphia to carry his views into execution . . . it occurred to him that by means of a common kite, he could have better access to the regions of thunder . . . dreading the ridicule which too commonly attends unsuccessful attempts in science, he communicated his intended experiment to nobody but his son . . . he observed some loose threads of the hempen string to stand erect . . . the discovery was complete. He perceived a very evident electrical spark . . . this happened . . . a month after the electricians in France had verified the same theory, but before he had heard of anything they had done," Priestley wrote.

Franklin wrote no scientific papers on the subject. His book was a compilation of letters written to Peter Collinson in London. Franklin reduced the mystery of electricity to its simplest terms and did not present scientific formulas, just facts, but, he made those facts interesting. He used his concise writing style to forward his research, an unheard-of practice in his day and even in today's scientific community.

"If my hypothesis is not the truth itself, it is at least as naked for all. . . . [I] have not . . . disguised my nonsense in Greek, clothed it in algebra or adorned it. . . ." Franklin wrote.

Peter Collinson was a fellow of the Royal Society of London. It was Collinson who provided Franklin with much of the electrical apparatus he needed to conduct his experiments, and he also reported to the Royal Society on Franklin's experiments. Collinson was responsible for having Franklin's letters published in book form.

Franklin's contributions to the scientific study of electricity were of major proportion. Having only had two years of formal education, he received honorary degrees from Harvard, Yale, and William and Mary in America, and he was inducted into the Royal Academy in London, because of his discoveries in the field of electrical science.

Ben Franklin was America's first "world citizen." He personified the true genius of America. He was an accomplished author, inventor, scientist, and statesman, and became known as the man who "snatched the lightning from the sky and the scepter from the tyrant." Among his publications, he is known for *Poor Richard's Almanack*, calendars surrounded by thought-provoking information and humor, which he published for twenty-five years and which were the most popular almanacs in America.

He wrote his *Autobiography*, which was started in 1771 and left unfinished at his death in 1790. It stands even today as the model of the hard-fought success of a true American and contributed to American literature an enduring style of clear, concise prose.

As an inventor, he was responsible for the Franklin stove, which set a new standard for efficiency, bifocals, the lightning rod, and Franklin chair, among a host of other contributions.

Although initially not in favor of the American Revolution, Franklin helped draft the Declaration of Independence, and served as ambassador to France during the Revolution, where he was able to provide the American rebels with French weapons and money. He helped to draft the peace treaty with England after the war.

Franklin established America's first public library, city hospital, and fire department. He printed one of America's first political cartoons and helped establish what is now the University of Pennsylvania.

Born in Boston, Massachusetts, in January 1706 and denied a formal education because of his family's poverty, Franklin went on to become one of America's most acclaimed citizens.

Benjamin Franklin died in Philadelphia at eighty-four years of age on April 17, 1790.

4 Thomas Paine (1737–1809)
Common Sense, 1776

"These are the times that try men's souls."

THE TIMES: The Universalist Church was established in America. Congress adopted the "Stars and Stripes" as the official flag of the country. The Declaration of Independence was first published in the *Pennsylvania Evening Post*. Esek Hopkins was appointed the first commander in chief of the Continental Navy. Patrick Henry delivered his famous "Give me liberty or give me death" speech in Virginia. Women's corsets were first introduced in America.

During the darkest days of the American Revolution, the country looked to a writer, Thomas Paine, for courage and inspiration.

After leaving England for America in 1774, Paine, with his rebellious writings, inspired colonists to the brink of the American Revolution and beyond. Following the bloody confrontation between American colonists and English troops at Lexington and Concord, Paine began his career as one of America's greatest political pamphleteers.

In January 1776, with the help of Philadelphia physician Benjamin Rush, also an outspoken advocate for American independence, Paine published *Common Sense*, a forty-seven-page pamphlet that argued that America's future demanded independence from England.

Paine's powerful language and eloquent call for American liberty made the pamphlet an immediate success. Historians have called it the most brilliant call to arms written during the American Revolution. Paine intended the pamphlet for a mass audience. It was aimed at forcing those colonists who were wavering on the issue of independence to join in the cause of liberty. He called the conflict with England a battle between good and evil and justified American independence as the will of the people. America's prosperity and progress, he asserted, demanded immediate independence from English rule.

"It is repugnant to reason, to the universal order of things, to all examples from former ages, to suppose that this continent can remain subject to any external power.

"We have the power to begin the world over again."
"The cause of America is in great measure the cause of all mankind."

Paine's rousing words were on the lips of every independence-minded colonist, and the reaction to *Common Sense* was immediate and far-reaching. Paine boasted that the success of the pamphlet was ". . . beyond anything since the invention of printing." More than 150,000 copies of the pamphlet were published, an extraordinary number, and it sold out immediately. Subsequently, twenty-five editions of it were published. It became the most influential publication of the times. John Adams predicted that Paine's writings would become "the common faith" of the land. George Washington called it "Sound doctrine and unanswerable."

Margaret Fuller (1810–50)

14 *Woman in the Nineteenth Century,* 1845

"As men become aware that all men have not had their fair chance, they are inclined to say that no women have had a fair chance."

THE TIMES: James Polk was elected president. Charles Goodyear discovered vulcanized rubber. Samuel Morse sent the first telegraph message from Washington, D.C., to Baltimore. "What hath God wrought?" was the message sent. The phrase "manifest destiny" appeared for the first time in an American political magazine. The first rotary press was built. It could publish eight thousand newspapers in an hour. It was first installed at the *Philadelphia Public Ledger.* America's first baseball game was played at Elysian Field in Hoboken, New Jersey.

One of America's most influential writers of the nineteenth century, Margaret Fuller, died in a shipwreck off the Long Island, New York, coast in July 1850, tragically cutting short what many believed would have been an astronomical literary career.

Lost in the shipwreck along with Fuller was her husband, Angelo Ossoli, an Italian revolutionary, and her two-year-old son, Nino. Fuller, who had the opportunity to save herself in one of the first rescue boats to reach the sinking ship, refused to leave her husband and child and chose instead to go down with the vessel. Their bodies were never recovered.

Fuller and her family had fled back to America following the unsuccessful defense of Rome by revolutionaries against the French in 1848–49. The revolutionaries, led by Giuseppe Mazzini, were intent on creating a Roman Republic, in revolt against the corrupt and cruel government of the Papal States. Fuller had served side by side with her husband during the siege of Rome, caring for the sick and wounded at an emergency hospital.

It was during this eventful period that Fuller completed what she felt was the most important work of her lifetime — a history of the Roman revolution. This unpublished manuscript was lost at sea in the shipwreck.

At the time of her death at the age of forty, Fuller had already left behind an unrivaled body of work and contributions to American society. Her book *Woman in the Nineteenth Century*, published in 1845, was one of the first books to advocate equal rights for women. It subsequently became an American classic on women's rights and the foundation of the modern American feminist movement. *Woman in the Nineteenth Century* served as the focal point at the Seneca Falls Convention of 1848 — the first organized women's rights convention. It was from this convention that the demand for women's suffrage was born.

Woman in the Nineteenth Century was a bold, ground-breaking work calling for economic, political, social, and sexual emancipation for American women. In it, Fuller advocated economic opportunity for women, full political rights, including the right to vote, and, most shocking of all, sexual freedom and equality. Fuller directly challenged the male-dominated social structure of the country, promoting agitation as a means of achieving equal rights and justice. She saw no position that could not be filled by a woman because of lack of ability.

"If you ask what offices [women] may fill, I reply – any," she wrote.

The book was the outgrowth of a series of meetings held in Boston from 1839 to 1844. Periodically, a group of women, led by Fuller, met to discuss issues of the time – among them equal rights for women. In 1843, Fuller published an essay in *The Dial*, the magazine of the American Transcendental movement, called "The Great Lawsuit. Man versus Men. Woman versus Women," which served as the foundation for the book published two years later.

Fuller served as the editor of *The Dial* from 1840 to 1842, during which time the small publication (it never had more than three hundred subscribers) became one of the most influential magazines in the country. It was the contention of Fuller, as one of the leading female figures in the American Transcendental movement, that her work as both a writer and editor was to "stimulate each man to judge for himself."

Besides editing the most influential magazine in the country and writing the leading book on women's rights, Fuller had the distinction of being the country's first professional newspaperwoman and the first female foreign correspondent for a major American newspaper.

Horace Greeley (1811–72), America's outspoken antislavery advocate and editor of the *New York Tribune*, invited Fuller to New York to work for him. She served as a reporter and later became a leading literary critic for the newspaper.

According to Greeley, she was "the most remarkable and in some respect the greatest woman whom America has yet known."

In 1846, Greeley sent Fuller to Europe to become the

first woman foreign correspondent. Her reports from abroad appeared regularly in the front pages of the *New York Tribune*. It was while she was in Europe that she became sympathetic to the Italian revolutionary cause and met Angelo Ossoli. She joined Ossoli in the struggle for the Roman Republic, and subsequently they became lovers. A year before they were married, she gave birth to their son, Nino. It was a radical departure for Fuller, who was born in Cambridgeport, Massachusetts, in May 1810 into a blue-blood family. Her father, Thomas, held many elected positions in the state.

She was educated at an early age in the classics — she begun Latin at the age of six — and as a teenager attended school in Groton, Massachusetts, where she mastered French, Italian, and Greek. An avid reader, she had free rein in her father's massive library and easily engaged in the discussion of philosophy with adults.

In 1835, Fuller was introduced to Ralph Waldo Emerson (1803–82) and became active in the Transcendental movement. She taught school for a time in Providence, Rhode Island, before returning to Boston, where she became the editor of *The Dial*. Emerson called her ". . . a fine . . . inspiring . . . eloquent talker, who did not outlive her influence."

Fuller found even Transcendentalism too confining for her. "Why bind oneself to a central or any doctrine? How much nobler stands a man entirely unpledged, unbound?" she wrote. She drifted away from the Boston Transcendental movement to the New York literary scene following Horace Greeley's overtures.

Fuller's need to grow intellectually and politically prompted her many moves — ultimately leading her to the Italian revolutionary cause. "Very early I knew that the only object in life was to grow," she wrote.

She had intended *Woman in the Nineteenth Century* as a

living document that would be updated and continually revised throughout her lifetime. This, however, was not to be the case.

Her untimely death robbed America of one of its greatest women writers. A memorial is erected in memory of Margaret Fuller and her family at Mount Auburn Cemetery in Cambridge, Massachusetts.

Frederick Douglass (1817–95)

15 Narrative of the Life of Frederick Douglass, 1845

"To the freedmen was given the machinery of liberty, but there was denied to them the steam to put it in motion."

THE TIMES: "Susanna," by Stephen Foster, was the most popular song in the country. The first American postage stamps were issued. The first American sewing machine was invented by Elias Howe. Horse racing was America's favorite sport. The first bridal suite was introduced at a New York City hotel. The Smithsonian Institution was established in Washington, D.C. Charles Webber, a former Texas Ranger, became one of America's most popular writers for his series of western novels.

Frederick Douglass's book *Narrative of the Life of Frederick Douglass* (1845) was published over the objections of the country's leading abolitionists, despite the fact that Douglass was America's leading antislavery advocate.

Abolitionists believed that because Douglass identified himself as a former slave and fugitive, he would lose his effectiveness as a lecturer. But publication of the book only enhanced Douglass's reputation, and he became the leading spokesman of the antislavery movement, lecturing throughout the North and England. Douglass used the money he earned from his speaking engagements to fund underground railroads to the North for Southern fugitive slaves.

Although there were many black antislavery writers and lecturers, none were as eloquent in both books and speeches as Douglass.

"Behold the practical operation of this internal slave-trade, the American slave-trade, sustained by American politics and American religion. Here you will see men and women, reared like swine, for the market. You know what is a swine drover? I will show you a man-drover. They inhabit all our Southern states," he wrote.

Douglass was born a slave in Maryland and was later sent to a plantation in Baltimore at the age of eight. While serving as a house servant, Douglass was taught to read and write — which was against the law at the time for slaves. At the age of sixteen, Douglass became a field hand and later a shipbuilding laborer. In 1838, when he was twenty-one, he disguised himself as a sailor and fled to New York City and then to New Bedford, Massachusetts, where as a fugitive slave, he hid from authorities.

In 1841, Douglass was invited to speak at an antislavery rally held on the island of Nantucket, Massachusetts. Although inexperienced at public speaking, Douglass delivered an emotionally charged speech depicting the horrors of slavery. His address was so eloquent that he was invited to become a lecturer for the Massachusetts Anti-Slavery Society.

Although he became one of the movement's most effective and sought-after speakers, he was nevertheless jeered and heckled. His enemies branded him a fraud, claiming he was merely a dupe for the antislavery movement. They claimed he was not a slave, but actually a free Northern black, educated and protected by his rarefied upbringing. His detractors refused to believe that any former slave could be as articulate as Douglass, whose fiery oratory and writing brought many people into the abolitionist movement.

"There is not a nation on Earth guilty of practices more shocking and bloody, than are the people of these United States, at this very hour," he said at an antislavery meeting in 1852.

In order to refute his detractors, Douglass wrote his auto-biography, *Narrative of the Life of Frederick Douglass*, in which he revealed his master's identity, putting his freedom at risk. Because of the book, he was forced to flee to England to avoid recapture by his former master.

He spent two years lecturing in England and Ireland. He returned to America with enough money to buy his freedom and also to start his own antislavery newspaper, the *North Star*. Douglass published the *North Star* from 1847 to 1860.

During the Civil War, he served as an adviser to President Lincoln. In this capacity, he strongly advocated that the war become a direct attack on the inhumane condition of slavery. He also advanced the idea of enlisting former slaves into the military service of the Northern cause.

After the war, he fought for civil rights for black Americans and for full social and economic freedom. His continued efforts led to the passage of the fourteenth and fifteenth amendments to the U.S. Constitution, guaranteeing blacks their freedom and their right to vote. Although the amendments guaranteed these rights, the government refused to enforce the laws. As in the antislavery movement and later during the Civil War, Douglass became an eloquent spokesman for the enforcement of the Constitutional guarantees.

"How stands the case with the recently emancipated mil-lions of colored people in our own country? . . . the Negro has been made free, made a citizen. . . . To this end, several amendments to the Constitution were proposed, recommended and adopted. . . . To the freedmen was given the machinery of liberty, but there was denied to them the steam to put it in motion. They were given the uniform of soldiers, but no arms; they were called citizens, but left subjects; they were called free, but left almost slaves," he wrote.

Douglass became the first black to hold a high-ranking position in the U.S. government. He held many positions, including that of U.S. minister to Haiti from 1889 to 1891.

Douglass rewrote *Narrative of the Life of Frederick Douglass* in 1855 as *My Bondage and My Freedom*. In 1881, he enlarged the autobiography into the book *The Life and Times of Frederick Douglass*. These books have become American classics.

Douglass died in 1895 in Washington, D.C., at the age of seventy-eight.

16 Henry David Thoreau (1817–62) "Civil Disobedience," 1849

"Why are you not here?"

THE TIMES: The first medical school for women was founded in Boston. The California Gold Rush began. Elizabeth Blackwell was the first woman in America to receive a medical degree. The first women's rights convention was held in Seneca Falls, New York. *The Scarlet Letter* was published by Nathaniel Hawthorne and became an immediate best-seller. Four thousand copies of the book were sold within a week of its publication. Herman Melville published *Moby Dick*, but it was nearly seventy years before it would be hailed as an American masterpiece. The *New York Times* newspaper was established.

It was more than six decades after it was first published that Henry David Thoreau's essay "Civil Disobedience" found an appreciative audience, and even then, it was not in America.

Unlike many publications that helped shape America, Thoreau's essay was not widely read when it was first published in 1849 and had little immediate impact. But in 1907, Mohandas Gandhi, then a young lawyer living in South Africa, discovered Thoreau's work and adopted "civil disobedience" as the cornerstone of his independence movement in India. "A friend sent me the essay on 'Civil Disobedience.' It left a deep impression upon me. . . . The essay seemed so convincing and truthful. . . ." Gandhi said. Gandhi was already practicing passive resistance in his struggle to rid his country of discriminating English laws. His interpretation of Thoreau's philosophy is found in the Hindu word "*satyagraha*," meaning the power of truth and nonviolence. Gandhi used Thoreau's theory of nonviolent resistance to ultimately gain India's independence from English rule.

During World War II, Thoreau's "Civil Disobedience" was the basis for the Danish resistance to the Nazis.

In 1945, the act of civil disobedience was upheld by the U.S. Supreme Court in a decision stating that "our Bill of Rights recognizes that in the domain of conscience there is a moral power higher than the state. . . ."

Thoreau's writing did not find a true following in America until the early 1960s, when his philosophy was adopted as the basis of the civil-rights movement led by the Reverend Martin Luther King, Jr. In King's hands, Thoreau's philosophy became a powerful force in overturning segregation laws and winning major concessions for the civil-rights movement.

King first read Thoreau's "Civil Disobedience" in 1944, while he was a student at Morehouse College in Atlanta, Georgia. According to King, he became "fascinated by the idea of refusing to cooperate with an evil system."

"When oppressed people willingly accept their oppression, they only serve to give the oppressor a convenient justification for his acts," King said.

Not everyone, however, found Thoreau's philosophy inspiring. U.S. senator Joseph McCarthy had copies of "Civil

Disobedience" banned from government libraries because they were, in his opinion, "un-American." Ironically, the two men who adopted and furthered Thoreau's philosophy of non-violence, Gandhi and King, both died violently, at the hands of assassins, Gandhi in 1948 and King in 1968.

Henry David Thoreau was born in Concord, Massachusetts, in 1817. He attended Harvard College (Harvard University) and graduated in 1837. He worked as a teacher in a Concord public school, but was dismissed for refusing to hand out discipline to students. In 1838, he began his own school with his brother. It lasted three years.

Considered a harmless eccentric by many of his Concord neighbors, Thoreau built a small cabin at Walden Pond where he lived alone and began writing his famous book *Walden*, published in 1854. The land at Walden Pond where he built his cabin was owned by his friend and mentor, Ralph Waldo Emerson (1803–82).

In 1846, Thoreau protested America's war with Mexico and the government's inaction on the issue of slavery by refusing to pay his taxes. Although his family and friends offered to pay his taxes, Thoreau refused to allow this compromise and was ultimately arrested. Maintaining that his protest was based on moral grounds, he went to jail, where he spent only one night. His taxes and fines were paid by an unidentified benefactor. When Emerson confronted Thoreau at the Concord jail and asked why he was in there, Thoreau reportedly remarked that a better question was "Why are you not here?" Thoreau was angered at Emerson's refusal to protest slavery more strenuously.

Thoreau used his brief stint in jail as the basis of his essay on civil disobedience. In it, he maintained that "government is best which governs not at all." According to Thoreau, "Government is at best but an expedient; but most governments are usually, and all governments are sometimes inexpedient.

"This American government, — what is it but a tradition, though a recent one, endeavoring to transmit itself unimpaired to posterity, but each instant losing some of its integrity?" he wrote.

He did not advocate an end to all government — "not at once no government, but at once a better government."

His contention was that an individual's conscience was the only basis for determining right and wrong. Mankind, he asserted, was answerable to a higher moral law than the laws written by governments: "any man more right than his neighbors constitutes a majority of one already."

He maintained that individuals had three choices of actions when it came to unjust laws — obey them; work to amend them; or openly resist them.

"Under a government which imprisons any unjustly, the true place for a just man is also a prison . . ." he wrote. Thoreau's ideas were not entirely original. The English legal writer William Blackstone was one of the first to advocate civil disobedience as a means of protest.

"Civil Disobedience" was originally published in May 1849 in Elizabeth Peabody's small publication *Aesthetic Papers*. It appeared under the title "Resistance to Civil Government." The essay received little notice when it first appeared and was not widely read, but it went on to become the basis for dramatic changes throughout America and the world.

Thoreau died in Concord in 1862 at the age of forty-five.

17 Harriet Beecher Stowe (1811–96)
Uncle Tom's Cabin, 1852

*"The little woman who wrote the book that
made this big war."*

THE TIMES: The first America's Cup sailing competition was held. The phrase "Go West, young man" was originated in an editorial by John B. L. Soule, editor of the *Terre Haute Express* newspaper. Franklin Pierce was elected president. "My Old Kentucky Home," by Stephen Foster, was the most popular song in the country. Gail Borden invented evaporated milk. The Republican party was formed. The hoop skirt was in fashion for women. The temperance novel *Ten Nights in a Barroom and What I Saw There*, by Timothy Arthur, was the second-best-selling book in the country next to *Uncle Tom's Cabin*.

Uncle Tom's Cabin was written in reverse order — beginning with the last chapter of the book!
   Harriet Beecher Stowe's 1852 novel *Uncle Tom's Cabin*, the most popular and influential book of the last century, was written after Stowe had a vision during a church service in Brunswick, Maine. According to Stowe, she saw the entire

ending of her unwritten book, the death of Uncle Tom at the hands of the villainous Simon Legree, appear before her eyes. After the service, Stowe went home and feverishly wrote the last chapter of the book.

"The Lord himself wrote it. I was but an instrument in His hand," Stowe said.

After she read the last chapter to her family, her husband, Calvin Stowe, a minister, and a professor at Bowdoin College, told her, "Begin at the beginning and work up to this and you'll have your book."

Stowe had vowed to write something powerful on the issue of slavery after moving back to New England from Cincinnati, where she had lived since 1832. She was compelled by her own revulsion at the passage of the Fugitive Slave Law in 1850, which allowed slave owners to recapture escaped slaves, even in states that prohibited slavery. She was spurred on by her sister-in-law, who pleaded with her to ". . . write something that would make the whole nation feel what an accursed thing slavery is."

While living in Cincinnati, Stowe had written and published several magazine stories. She contacted one of the editors she had known, Gamaliel Bailey, who was now the editor of *National Era*, an antislavery newspaper in Washington, D.C., about publishing *Uncle Tom's Cabin* in serial form. She informed Bailey that her story would run for three or four installments. "I shall show the best side of the thing, and something faintly approaching the worst," she told Bailey. Bailey paid her three hundred dollars for the serial rights of the book and began serializing it in June 1851, but Stowe's work ran on for more than forty installments and appeared in *National Era* from 1851 until April 1852. According to Bailey, no American writer ". . . excited more general and profound interest."

Stowe's book was published in March 1852 before the final installment appeared in *National Era*. It was published by a small Boston publishing house, John P. Jewett, after another Boston publisher, Phillips, Sampson and Company, had rejected it as being too controversial.

Even Jewett was apprehensive about the possible success of the book, based on its topic and the fact that it ran two volumes in length. Stowe was offered a 50–50 share of the book if she would consent to share in the production costs. Stowe refused the offer and accepted the standard 10 percent royalty. It was a decision that cost her millions of dollars.

Stowe was not sure the book would make any money and privately expressed to her husband that she hoped it would at least earn enough in royalties for her to purchase a new dress. The five thousand copies of the first edition sold out within two days — three thousand copies sold out on the day of publication and the rest the next day. After a month, Jewett had sold ten thousand copies, and by the end of the year three hundred thousand copies of *Uncle Tom's Cabin* had been sold in America. By 1857, nearly 500,000 copies of the book had been sold in America, and nearly a million copies were sold in England.

Since there weren't any international copyright laws, Stowe received no royalties from the sale of the book in England despite the fact that nearly twenty different London publishers issued copies of it. Versions of the book were translated into more than twenty languages, and it soon became a best-seller in Europe.

Although Stowe refused to give her permission to dramatize the book, *Uncle Tom's Cabin* soon became the most popular play in America. Hundreds of theater companies produced versions of the story. Again, because of copyright laws, Stowe did not receive any royalties from the theatrical versions of her book.

Nothing in America's publishing history equaled the success of *Uncle Tom's Cabin*, and in terms of sheer volume, nothing except the Bible ever surpassed the book's wide acceptance.

The financial success of the book was surpassed only by the impact it had on American culture and politics. The book laid bare the cruelty of slavery and served as an indictment of the American government and its laws condoning slavery. American poet Henry Wordsworth Longfellow hailed the novel as ". . . one of the greatest triumphs recorded in literary history. . . ." *Uncle Tom's Cabin* had such a powerful impact that when President Lincoln met Stowe for the first time, he referred to her as, "the little woman who wrote the book that made this big war."

According to Stowe, she had written the book in an attempt to avoid war between the states. She had written it, she said, "to soften and moderate the bitterness of feeling in extreme abolitionists . . . to inspire free colored people with self-respect, hope and confidence."

Although she tried to present a fair view of Southern slave owners, Southern critics immediately denounced the novel. *Uncle Tom's Cabin* was called "criminal prostitution of the highest functions of imagination" by the *Southern Literary Messenger*. Stowe was accused of making up the so-called "facts" in the book, and thousands of protest letters were sent to the offices of *National Era*. Nearly thirty anti–Uncle Tom books were published, refuting Stowe's work, and some Southerners were sent to jail for having the book in their possession.

In the North, businessmen denounced the book, fearing it endangered their Southern business investments. Many people condemned it, even if they disagreed with slavery, because they feared it would only cause more unrest. The London *Times* said the book was "engendering ill will, keeping up bad blood."

In 1853, Stowe published *A Key to Uncle Tom's Cabin*, in

which she cited the factual sources of her book. The sources included newspaper accounts, court records, and laws, and cited the book *American Slavery as It Is*, published in 1839 by Theodore Weld (1803–95). "It is made up of the facts, the documents, the things which my own eyes have looked upon," Stowe wrote.

The immense popularity of *Uncle Tom's Cabin* is not attributed merely to Stowe's indictment of slavery. There simply were not enough abolitionists or antislavery sympathizers in America at the time it was published to turn it into such a tremendous best-seller.

Over the years, critics have called the book melodramatic and sentimental. Some have noted how poorly written it was. But it contained all the high emotional elements of suspense, love, murder, lust, humor, and human tragedy to successfully engage a wide reading audience. Stowe wrote only one more antislavery book in her lifetime, *Dred, A Tale of the Great Dismal Swamp*. Published in 1856, it never achieved the fame of *Uncle Tom's Cabin*.

Born in Litchfield, Connecticut, in 1811, Harriet Beecher Stowe attended Litchfield Academy. In 1832, she moved with her family to Cincinnati. In 1836, she married Calvin Stowe. The Stowes had seven children. In 1850, Harriet Beecher Stowe moved to Maine, where she began work on *Uncle Tom's Cabin*. Following the success of the book, she spent the rest of her life writing, averaging nearly a book a year. Among her other books were *The Pearl of Orr's Island* (1862), *Oldtown Folks* (1869), and *Poganuc People* (1878).

She died in Florida in 1896 at the age of eighty-five.

18 Abraham Lincoln (1809–65)
The Gettysburg Address, 1863

*"It is for us the living, rather to be dedicated
here to the unfinished work which they who
fought here have thus far so nobly advanced."*

THE TIMES: Theodore Winthrop, who was killed in the beginning days of the Civil War, was one the country's most popular writers when a collection of his western novels were published posthumously, among them the novel *John Brent*. President Lincoln issued the Emancipation Proclamation. General Robert E. Lee led Southern forces into Pennsylvania, where he lost the decisive battle of Gettysburg. *The Man Without a Country*, by Edward Everett Hale, became a best-seller. Roller skating was introduced into American society. The phrase "In God We Trust" first appeared on American coins. Lee surrendered at Appomattox Courthouse in Virginia, bringing the Civil War to an end. President Abraham Lincoln was assassinated at Ford's Theatre in Washington, D.C.

It has been estimated that Abraham Lincoln, the country's sixteenth president, composed over one million words in his various speeches and publications. It is ironic then, that of all the words he spoke or wrote, he is perhaps best remembered for the very shortest thing he composed, the Gettysburg Address.

It is even more ironic that portions of this memorable speech, which is only ten sentences long, actually contain someone else's words — those of Unitarian minister Theodore Parker of Massachusetts. Lincoln used Parker's words almost verbatim.

The lines in question are the very last lines, beginning with the words "that this nation, under God, shall have a new birth of freedom — and that government of the people, by the people and for the people, shall not perish from this earth." In one of Parker's famous published sermons, "A Sermon of Merchants," delivered in November 1846, he stated, "government is of all, by all, and for all. . . ." These compelling words became part of Lincoln's most stirring speech.

Plagiarism aside, it was a logical association for Lincoln, "the Great Emancipator," to paraphrase a man who dedicated his life to preaching freedom for slaves. As a young lawyer in Illinois, Lincoln was an avid reader of Theodore Parker. His sermons were regularly reprinted in the country's newspapers. "Theodore Parker is my kind of Christian," Lincoln once said.

In his lifetime, Parker (1810–60) was called "the Great American Preacher." He preached regularly every Sunday from the Music Hall in Boston, where close to two thousand people came each week to hear him. Whenever slave owners traveled to Boston to reclaim their runaway slaves, Parker would leaflet the city with posters warning slaves. He was once arrested for helping a slave escape, but after he prepared a written defense consisting of more than 250 pages, the charges against him were dropped.

Regardless of Theodore Parker's uncredited contribution to the Gettysburg Address, this famous speech delivered by

President Lincoln on November 19, 1863, stands as one of the most inspiring and memorable documents in American history.

Although the speech was given to dedicate the cemetery at Gettysburg, Pennsylvania, it stands today, not as homage to the Union's military victory, but as a poetic tribute to all those who sacrificed their lives preserving the democratic ideals of the country. It was a call to the American people to dedicate themselves to the principles that the Union soldiers at Gettysburg fought and died for.

Lincoln's address was delivered four months after the crucial Union victory at Gettysburg. The battle, fought on July 3, 1863, was a turning point in the war for the Union forces. General Robert E. Lee had advanced his troops into Pennsylvania in a strategic gamble to divide the Union forces and attack them in their own territory — hopefully bringing about a swift end to the war and victory for the Confederates. This was not to be.

In one of the bloodiest battles of the Civil War, the Confederate Army lost close to thirty thousand soldiers, while Union troops suffered a little more than twenty-thousand casualties. The Confederate forces were beaten back, and Lee withdrew his army. The Southern forces never again fought on Northern territory. Although it was a high price for both armies to pay, the Union Army was able to claim victory.

When Lincoln came to dedicate a cemetery at the site of the battlefield some four months later, he was not scheduled as the main speaker for the dedication ceremony. Edward Everett (1794–1865), a noted orator and clergyman, gave the keynote address. Everett's lengthy discourse was more than two hours long. It was reprinted in many of the country's major newspapers and took up two newspaper-sized sheets of paper. Not a single phrase of Everett's speech is remembered today, while

Lincoln's five-minute address stands today as one of the most often quoted and memorable speeches in the world.

Prior to giving his famous speech, Lincoln was asked by a newspaper reporter how his own speech would compare to Edward Everett's discourse. Lincoln replied that in comparison, his would be "short, short, short."

Abraham Lincoln was born in 1809, near Hodgenville, Kentucky. True to the myths surrounding him, he was born in a log cabin. He later moved to Illinois.

As a child, he had wanted to become a writer. In one of the notebooks he kept as a boy, he wrote, "Abraham Lincoln his hand and pen, he will be good, but God knows when." Although he had a meager formal education, Lincoln was a voracious reader and often traveled distances to borrow books. Among his favorites were *Pilgrim's Progress*, *History of the United States*, and *The Life of Washington*.

Before entering politics, he held many jobs. He was a surveyor, storekeeper, and woodcutter. He ultimately settled on practicing law and, finally, politics.

Lincoln was not an entirely successful politician. He ran for the United States Senate and lost; he was rejected for a top government position; and he ran for the vice presidency and was defeated. He tried business but failed at that too. He was elected to the Illinois House of Representatives in 1834 and was reelected several times. In 1846, he was finally elected to Congress, but served without distinction. In 1854, when the Republican party was founded, Lincoln became one of its most active proponents.

In the presidential campaign of 1860, Lincoln was pitted against the lawyer and legislator Stephen A. Douglas (1813–61). When Douglas encouraged the extension of slavery in the South, Lincoln challenged him to the now-famous Lincoln-Douglas debates. It was during these debates that Lincoln set forth his philosophy on the state of the Union: "This government cannot endure permanently half slave and half free," he proclaimed.

Although Douglas mocked Lincoln's stand and proclaimed that his opponent was not of national-government caliber, Lincoln went on to win the election by half a million votes. In response to Lincoln's election, North Carolina seceded from the Union. When Lincoln finally took office in March of 1861, the country was on the brink of civil war.

Perhaps the biggest irony surrounding the Gettysburg Address is that Lincoln himself placed little faith in the lasting impact of the speech, telling the audience, "The world will little note, nor long remember what we say here . . ." How very wrong he was.

19 Elizabeth Peabody (1804–94)
Kindergarten Culture, 1870

*"Is it not better to make men and women,
than to make books?"*

THE TIMES: *Little Women* by Louisa May Alcott was published and sold more than 2 million copies. The typewriter was invented. Arabella Mansfield became the first woman lawyer in America. Mark Twain published *The Innocents Abroad*. Thomas Nast introduced the donkey as the symbol of the Democratic party. James McNeill Whistler exhibited his painting "Whistler's Mother" for the first time.

One of the most far-reaching developments in American education — the establishment of the kindergarten system — was set in motion by a woman who had no children of her own.

Elizabeth Peabody, who was born in Billerica, Massachusetts, in 1804, began the first American kindergarten on Pickney Street in Boston in 1860. "Kindergartening," she wrote in *Kindergarten Culture*, one of her many books on early childhood education, "is not a craft, it is a religion; not an avocation, but a vocation from on high." Although she can be credited with starting the first kindergarten, it was her writings and lectures that most contributed to the establishment of the kindergarten system throughout the country. And it was through her devotion to this cause that the first "public" kindergarten was founded.

Although she founded the Pickney Street Kindergarten in 1860, Peabody was not satisfied that her understanding of early childhood education was sufficient. Her interest in kindergartens came from reading the works of the German educator Friedrich Froebel, considered to be the "Father of Kindergarten Education." It was because of his writings that she became devoted to Froebel's principle of "creative self-activity" in early childhood education and made it her life's work.

In 1867, wanting to learn more about Froebel's teachings, she traveled to Germany, where she visited established kindergartens and studied with people who had known Froebel. After her return to America, Peabody declared her Pickney Street Kindergarten a failure because it did not adhere to Froebel's teachings and closed the school.

In her absence, another kindergarten had been established in Boston under the direction of Peabody's younger sister Mary. She was the wife of America's most renowned educator, Horace Mann. There were three sisters in the Peabody family: Elizabeth, the oldest, Mary, and Sophia. Mary, who was a well-respected teacher and innovator, married Horace Mann, while Sophia Peabody married Nathaniel Hawthorne, one of America's literary giants.

With the establishment of a genuine kindergarten in Boston under the leadership of her sister, Peabody devoted herself to writing and lecturing on the subject of kindergarten education. She published *Kindergarten Messenger*, an independent journal promoting educational reform, as well as numerous books, including *Kindergarten Culture* (1870) and *Letters to Kindergarteners* (1886). She traveled extensively throughout America, lecturing tirelessly on the subject and promoting the establishment of kindergartens throughout the country.

Although the first publicly financed kindergarten in Boston failed after four years because of lack of public appropriations, Elizabeth Peabody did not curtail her efforts, and ultimately kindergartens, both publicly and privately financed, sprang up across the country.

Peabody's own early education came from her mother, of whom she wrote, "There is nothing for which I thank my mother and my God more than for this grand impression of all inspiring love for God, and for all-conquering duty to posterity, thus made on my childish imagination and its association with the idea of personal freedom and independent action."

Later, her more formal education came from attending Bronson Alcott's progressive Temple School. Alcott was an American educator, philosopher, and author of *Concord Days* (1872). His innovations in education did not catch on with the public, and the Temple School ultimately closed. Peabody recorded her experience at the Temple School in her book *Record of a School* (1835).

After leaving the Temple School, she became active in adult education in Boston and taught history. Before becoming a tireless advocate of kindergarten education, Peabody was an integral part of the golden age of literature and philosophy in Boston, then considered the "Athens of America."

In 1839, she opened a bookstore on West Street, which became the gathering place for many of the greatest minds in America, among them, Margaret Fuller, Hawthorne, Mann, William Channing, and Julia Ward Howe.

Peabody was one of the planners of and participants in the Brook Farm experiment — one of the first utopian communities, founded in West Roxbury, Massachusetts, in 1841. She was, along with Margaret Fuller, one of the leading women in America's Transcendental movement. She wrote and edited *The Dial*, the movement's literary publication, and on her own printing press she published the early works of Fuller and Hawthorne.

However, Peabody gave up what many considered a promising literary career when she made kindergartens her calling.

Moncure Conway, a noted journalist of the time and chronicler of the works of Thomas Paine, said of her, "Miss Peabody's devotion to kindergarten is one of the great literary tragedies. She could be one of the great women of letters in America."

In response to this, Peabody countered, "Is it not better to make men and women, than to make books?"

Peabody spread the gospel of Froebel's kindergarten philosophy, which advocated play as a basic form of self-expression, wherever she could find an audience, and wrote frequently about his theories in many of the magazines and journals of the period. She firmly believed that Froebel's theories were a way of expanding human horizons and dedicated herself completely to this cause.

It was said of Miss Peabody that her thoughts were so filled with ideas and plans about spreading the gospel of kindergartens throughout the country, she often neglected the formalities of normal daily living. To many, her behavior appeared eccentric. According to Lucy Wheelock, an early kindergarten teacher who accompanied Peabody on several speaking engagements around the country, the unassuming Peabody was in the habit of wearing her nightgown under her dress, and she carried her toothbrush in her pocket, mindful that she might be called upon to lecture somewhere and wanting to be prepared to leave on a moment's notice, unencumbered by bag or baggage. She is thought to be the model for the character of Miss Peabody in the novel *The Bostonians* by Henry James.

In her later years, she became an outspoken advocate of Indian rights, and her last few public-speaking engagements were for the purpose of pleading for justice for the American Indian.

Elizabeth Peabody died at the age of ninety years old and is buried in the Sleepy Hollow Cemetery in Concord, Massachusetts. Her epitaph reads: *A teacher of three generations of children and the founder of the kindergarten in America. Every human cause had her sympathy and man her active aid.*

Indeed, although Elizabeth Peabody had no children of her own, it can be truly said that every child in America was her child.

20 Henry George (1839–97)
Progress and Poverty, 1879

> *"This association of poverty with progress is the great enigma of our times."*

THE TIMES: Thomas Edison invented the phonograph. Yellow fever claimed nearly fourteen thousand lives across the nation. Women lawyers won the right to argue cases before the Supreme Court. Madison Square Garden was opened in New York City. Edison Electric Light Company, the first electric-light company, was founded. Henry James published *Daisy Miller,* and Frank Woolworth began his chain of department stores.

One of the most powerful and influential American books on economics was written by a man who once begged on the streets of San Francisco for enough money to feed his starving family.

"I walked along the street and made up my mind to get money from the first man whose appearance might indicate he had it to give," said Henry George, author of the book *Progress and Poverty,* which was published in 1879.

According to George, a stranger gave him five dollars.

"If he had not, I think I was desperate enough to have killed him," he said.

Out of work, with no prospects in sight and a wife and family to support, George knew well the plight of the poor. Years later, when he wrote his famous book on American economics, he did not forget what it was like to be poor, and what steps needed to be taken to lift the poor from their economic misery. *Progress and Poverty* almost single-handedly popularized the sagging science of economics in America. George wrote in a way the public could understand, and he designed an economic theory that appealed to the masses. It was a powerful combination.

George contended that the private ownership of land was the basis of poverty in America and that it stood in the way of the country's overall economic progress. He proposed that industrial growth and progress fed into the cycle of poverty by increasing rents and thereby lowering wages.

"Why, in spite of increases in productive power, do wages tend to a minimum, which will give but a bare living?" George asked.

It was morally wrong, he contended, for landowners to become wealthy simply because they had the good luck to own property. He proposed the nationalization of all land and a single property tax that would absorb all rent. According to George, all other forms of taxation would be abolished with the advent of a single land tax — "with the growth in population, land grows in value, and the men who work it must pay more for the privilege."

He did not believe that anyone should benefit financially simply through the ownership of land. He contended that all working men and women had an equal right to use land for the basis of production. According to George, industrialists deserved whatever financial reward they could reap for rendering services or creating products.

Through his single-tax program, George maintained that wages would rise, because there would be no increasing rents, and with more land readily available, more goods and products would be produced. This increase in production would lead to more jobs and ultimately the eradication of all poverty.

George had very little formal education and was for the most part self-educated in the field of economics. He wrote *Progress and Poverty* over a period of nineteen months. After sending the completed manuscript to more than a dozen publishers, who all turned it down, George privately printed five hundred copies of the book.

A friend, William Hinton, who owned a printing company, agreed to make up the printing plates for the book. The publisher, D. Appleton and Company in New York, which had initially rejected the book, agreed to publish it commercially, since the overhead costs of making the printing plates had already been paid for. Appleton published the book in 1880.

The publishers had such little faith in the potential financial success of the book that they did not bother to copyright it for foreign sales, yet *Progress and Poverty* became an overnight success. Two million copies of the book sold in America, and it was translated into thirteen languages. It was the most widely read book before the turn of the century. Even to this day, close to ten thousand copies of the book sell yearly.

British dramatist George Bernard Shaw (1856–1950) said of George's book, "When I was then swept into the great Socialist revival of 1883, I found that five-sixths of those who were swept in with me had been converted by Henry George."

With the publication of *Progress and Poverty*, George became an international celebrity. People all over the world saw in George's theories true hope for a better world. He became a much sought-after lecturer and traveled extensively throughout America, England, Ireland, Canada, and Australia, promoting his single-tax theory.

The book outsold every other economic textbook of its day, to the chagrin of many academic economists. According to the California newspaper *The San Francisco Argonaut*, George's book was "the book of this half century." *The New York Tribune* proclaimed that *Progress and Poverty* had "no equal since the publication of *The Wealth of Nations* by Adam Smith."

Most American economists mocked the book, claiming it was the work of a publicity seeker and that it did not present a sound economic foundation. George countered that most economists in America were concerned only with maintaining the status quo of the wealthy and undermining the poor.

"For the study of political economy, you need no specific knowledge, no extensive library, no costly laboratory. You do not even need textbooks nor teachers, if you will but think for yourself," George said.

And the American reading public did think for themselves, and what they thought was that Henry George had a great idea. George's work became a serious threat to the American economists. Their dull textbooks, usually rehashing the same old economic theories, were seldom read, except by other economists. George, on the other hand, became quoted throughout American households. Clubs advocating George's theories sprang up all across America and in England. His ideas, in abbreviated versions, were adopted by American leaders, including President Woodrow Wilson. His enemies called him "the apostle of anarchy and destruction."

"A great wrong always dies hard and the great wrong which in every civilized country condemns the masses of men to poverty and want, will not die without a bitter struggle," George said.

Because of George's fame and popularity, he was drafted to run for mayor of New York City in 1886. George was not able to translate his popularity as an author into votes. In a three-way race, he was defeated by the corrupt Tammany Hall–appointed candidate. George ran second, defeating the Republican candidate, Teddy Roosevelt.

Henry George was born in September 1839 in Philadelphia, Pennsylvania. At the age of fifteen, he became a merchant seaman and traveled the world. He settled in San Francisco, where he went to work first as a printer and later as a newspaper reporter. In 1871, he helped found and later edited *The San Francisco Evening Post*. He later sold his interest in the paper for a loss. He worked as a free-lance writer for several years, living in dire poverty.

In 1887, he was persuaded to run for mayor of New York City for the second time. He was already in poor health but accepted the challenge. Four days before the election, he suffered a stroke and died on October 29, 1897.

More than one hundred thousand people paid their respects at his funeral.

21 Helen Hunt Jackson
A Century of Dishono

"They will live on and wil

THE TIMES: Lew Wallace published *Ben Hur*. The Sherwin-Williams Company in Ohio began to manufacture house paint. President James Garfield was assassinated, and Chester Arthur became president. *Uncle Remus* was published by Joel Chandler Harris, and the American Red Cross was founded. "The Lady or the Tiger," a short story by Frank Stockton, appeared for the first time in *Century Magazine*. It went on to become a literary favorite in national anthologies. The outlaw Jesse James was shot in the back and killed by Robert Ford, a member of his own gang.

The American Indians lost everything — their lands and heritage — entire tribes were wiped off the face of the earth they loved so much. It seems appropriate, then, that Helen Hunt Jackson would become the author of one of the most passionate and influential indictments of the American government's treatment of the American Indian. Jackson was no stranger to loss.

Her book, *A Century of Dishonor*, published in 1881, detailed the government's long history of broken promises and treaties with the Indians and helped lead the way to national reforms.

Jackson, who was born in Amherst, Massachusetts, in 1830 and was a friend and neighbor of poet Emily Dickinson, lost her entire family. Her husband, a major in the army corps of engineers, died in an accident while testing an underwater submarine device he had invented. Her first child died before he was a year old. Her remaining child died from diphtheria in 1865.

Jackson turned to writing to overcome her grief. Three months after her son's death, she published her first poem in *The Nation*. Her first volume of poetry was published in 1870. She wrote under various pseudonyms and signed her poetic works "H.H." (Helen Hunt). In 1875, she married a Quaker banker, William Jackson, and moved to Colorado with him. She was a prolific writer, turning out numerous volumes of prose and poetry, novels, plays, and children's stories. Her work appeared in the leading magazines and newspapers in the country.

Jackson admitted that she was not by nature a reformist, but after attending a lecture in Boston given by several members of the Ponca Indian tribe, she found herself outraged at the atrocities committed against American Indians and resolved to do something about it. She spent months researching Indian affairs, poring over documents and reports, the details of which she called a "sickening record of murder, outrage, robbery and wrongs."

A Century of Dishonor was a five-hundred-page exposé of the government's brutal mistreatment of the American Indians. At the time of its publication, nearly all the tribes were confined to reservations.

"There is not among these three hundred bands of Indians,

one which has not suffered cruelly at the hands of either the government or of white settlers," Jackson wrote.

The book was published between blood-red covers, and at her own expense she sent copies of it to every member of Congress.

"Cheating, robbing, breaking promises — these are clearly things which must cease to be done. One more thing, also, and that is the refusal of the protection of the law to the Indian's rights of property, of life, liberty, and the pursuit of happiness," she wrote.

The book stirred a passionate national debate on the issue of Indian relations. Widely read, it initially produced some minor reforms. In 1882, the Indian Rights Association was created to help improve the conditions of the Indians, and in 1883 the Lake Mohawk Conference of Friends of Indians was held to promote the rights of Indians.

Jackson was awarded a commission by the U.S. Department of the Interior to study the conditions of the Mission Indians in California. After a year of study, she filed a report that denounced the economic and social oppression of the tribe: ". . . having become a custom to pay an Indian only half the wages of a white man," she reported.

Jackson's report produced few results in Washington, but this did not stop her. She was determined to write a book, she said, that would do for American Indians what *Uncle Tom's Cabin* did for slaves.

"If I can do one-hundredth part for the Indians as Mrs. Stowe did for the Negroes, I will be thankful," Jackson said.

In 1884, she wrote *Ramona*, a romantic novel about California's victimized Indians. Although the book was both critically acclaimed and commercially successful, it did not produce the results Jackson had intended. The American reading public was more interested in it as a romantic novel than as a plea for reform. *Ramona* went on to be published in more than three hundred editions and several successful movie versions.

It was not until two years after Jackson's death that *A Century of Dishonor* and *Ramona* produced any effective changes in Indian affairs. In 1887, the Dawes Severalty Act was passed by Congress, giving the president the authority to distribute Indian lands among the tribes. It also allowed the president to award American citizenship to the Indians. Often referred to as the "Indian Emancipation Act," the act was the direct result of Jackson's books.

Despite an illustrious literary career, Jackson maintained that her two books on the American Indians were the only things she wrote that were of any worth. "They will live on and will bear fruit," she said. Jackson continued to write and promote the cause of Indian rights for the rest of her life. Just prior to her death, she had contacted President Grover Cleveland, urging him to further improve conditions for the Indians.

Jackson died at the age of fifty-four in 1885. She is buried in Colorado Springs. At the time of her death, she was considered the leading woman author in the country.

22 Emma Lazarus (1849–87) "The New Colossus," 1883

"Give me your tired, your poor,
Your huddled masses yearning to breathe
free . . ."

THE TIMES: The Brooklyn Bridge was opened. Mark Twain published *Life on the Mississippi*, followed by his most famous work, *Huckleberry Finn*. Lewis Waterman developed the fountain pen. The first night baseball game under electric lights was played in Indiana. Grover Cleveland was elected president. Buffalo Bill's Wild West Show toured throughout America and England.

Contrary to popular myth, America, the great melting pot, did not readily welcome immigrants with open arms. But American writers, notably Emma Lazarus with her stirring poem "The New Colossus," which appears on the base of the Statue of Liberty, did.

In 1884, Lazarus, a well-known poet of her day, wrote "The New Colossus" as part of a fund-raising effort to help finance the construction of the pedestal for the Statue of Liberty. The statue, designed by Frédéric-Auguste Bartholdi, was under construction in Paris when a prominent American civic group was formed to raise money to pay for the statue's base. A group of American writers and artists were commissioned to donate and auction off their work to help raise the funds.

Lazarus's sonnet was written to welcome European immigrants to the new world.

> "From her beacon head
> Glows world-wide welcome . . ."

In October 1886, the Statue of Liberty was dedicated by President Grover Cleveland. A gift of France, and intended as a symbol of America's hundred years of independence and to commemorate French and American friendship, the copper statue weighed 225 tons and stood 152 feet high.

Emma Lazarus's poem did not play a significant part in the dedication and received very little notice when it was first written. It wasn't until nearly twenty years after Lazarus's death in 1903 that the sonnet was engraved on a bronze plaque and placed inside the statue, where it languished unnoticed for another twenty-seven years.

> "The wretched refuse of your teeming shore,
> Send these, the homeless, tempest-tost to me,
> I lift my lamp beside the golden door."

Lazarus's noble sentiments were not shared by a majority of Americans during the great European exodus to America of the 1900s. To the contrary, efforts by the American public to stop the flow of immigrants into the country led to many restrictions, until in 1924 European immigration ground to a halt.

The persecution of the Jews in Nazi Germany during the

1930s brought the issue of immigration to the forefront of American debate. Through the efforts of an American journalist, Lazarus's poem was popularized during this period as a national statement on America's place as a safe haven for all the people of the world.

At the end of World War II, the bronze plaque engraved with Lazarus's poem was enshrined at the main entrance of the Statue of Liberty, as a testament to America's enduring promise of hope and freedom.

Lazarus had been an impassioned supporter of the Jewish people in her poetry and prose. She was a tireless organizer for relief efforts during the 1881 exodus of Jews out of Russia when thousands of Jewish refugees flooded into New York City. The persecution of Russian Jews during 1879–83 was a turning point for Lazarus. Until that time, she had not demonstrated any connection to her Jewish heritage. When asked once to contribute a poem to a Jewish songbook, she declined. "I feel no religious fervor within me," she said.

All that was to change dramatically.

When a Russian journalist wrote an article for *Century Magazine* in April 1882, defending the Russian persecution of the Jews, Lazarus responded with an article of her own condemning the conditions in Russia. Thereafter, she became known as an ardent champion of her people in both poetry and prose.

In 1882, she published *Songs of a Semite*, which contained poems and Hebrew translations. The book was intended to dramatize the plight of the Russian Jews and to help mobilize support. The book contained one of her most inspiring works, *The Dance to Death*, a verse play about fourteenth-century Jewish life that reaffirmed the spirit of the persecuted Jewish people.

"Even as we die in honor, from our death
Shall bloom a myriad of heroic lives . . ."

In her essays, most published in the *American Hebrew* magazine, Lazarus wrote about the history of the Jewish people, citing their contributions to the world and their persecution throughout history. In these early works, Lazarus had the foresight to call for the formation of a Jewish state.

In 1883, she traveled to England, where she was hailed as a champion of Jewish immigrants. She had by then acquired an international reputation. Returning to America, she wrote a series of poems for *Century Magazine*, "By the Waters of Babylon," and a series of articles, "An Epistle to the Hebrews," published in the *American Hebrew* magazine.

In 1885, she returned to England and spent the next two years traveling throughout Italy and France. Although best known as a champion of the Jewish people, Lazarus remained steadfast in her faith in America as the home for the downtrodden and oppressed of all races, ethnic groups, and religions.

She was born in New York City in 1849 into a wealthy and fashionable family and educated by private tutors. She published her first book of poetry when she was eighteen. The book, *Poems and Translations*, was privately printed in 1867 and contained material she had begun writing at fourteen. Although the poems were mostly youthful flights of romanticism, they displayed an unusual grasp of poetic structure, especially for someone so young.

The book attracted the attention of Ralph Waldo Emerson (1803–82), who was so taken by the poems that he invited Lazarus to visit him in Concord. Their friendship lasted her entire life.

In 1871, Lazarus published her second book of poetry,

Admetus and Other Poems, dedicating the book to Emerson. This new collection reflected far more maturity in her writing, as well as Emerson's influence. Included in this second collection was "Heroes," an ardent antiwar poem. She became a frequent contributor to many of the top publications of her day, including *Lippincott's Magazine*, *Century*, and *Scribner's*.

Lazarus was stricken with cancer while in England in 1887 and returned home to New York City, where she died at the age of thirty-eight in November 1887.

Her sonnet "The New Colossus," inscribed on the base of the Statue of Liberty, is a testament not only to American ideals, but to Emma Lazarus's uncompromising faith in America as the "Mother of Exiles."

23 Edward Bellamy (1850–98)
Looking Backward, 1888

"And in heaven's name, who are the public enemies? Are they France, England, Germany, or hunger, cold and nakedness?"

THE TIMES: The first golf club
Benjamin Harrison was elected presi
was used for the first time in nat
Thayer's poem "Casey at the Bat"
popular poem. The Kodak camera wa:
Eastman. The Johnstown Flood killed
people.

Edward Bellamy was an obscure New England writer and editor, but with the publication of his utopian novel *Looking Backward* in 1888, he became not only the best-selling author of his times, but the leader of the social-reform movement in America.

He was born in Chicopee Falls, Massachusetts, on March 26, 1850. His father was a Baptist minister in the town, and Edward went to public schools. Bellamy spent most of his life in Chicopee Falls, even after the success of his book.

He had a vivid imagination as a child and enjoyed reading,

mostly adventure stories and history. Although suffering from tuberculosis, he set his sights on the military, but was rejected by West Point because of his failing health. He attended one year of Union College, and then, at the age of eighteen, went to Europe. There, he first witnessed the terrible social and economic conditions confronting society.

"It was in the great cities of Europe that my eyes were first fully opened to the extent and consequences of man's inhumanity to man," Bellamy said.

Upon his return to America, he studied law. He was admitted to the bar in 1871, but chose not to practice. Instead, he went to work as a writer for the New York *Evening Post*. After a short stint there, he joined the Springfield (Massachusetts) *Union* as an editorial writer. He held the position for six years (1872–78), but his deteriorating health forced him to leave.

After a trip to Hawaii to recover from his illness, he returned and began his own newspaper in 1880, in partnership with his brother Charles. He stayed with the newly formed Springfield *Daily News* for two years. In 1882, he left the newspaper to devote full time to writing.

During this period, he married Emma Sanderson of Chicopee Falls. He and his wife moved into a house next door to his parents. Two years later, the Bellamys had a son, and two years after that, Emma gave birth to a daughter.

Bellamy produced a series of romantic novels, among them, *Six to One: A Nantucket Idyll* (1878); *The Duke of Stockbridge* (1879), which was originally serialized in the *Berkshire Courier* newspaper; *Dr. Heidenhoff's Process* (1880), and *Miss Ludington's Sister* (1884). Reviewers of these early works likened him to Nathaniel Hawthorne and referred to him as a "genteel romantic." But in 1888, with the publication of *Looking Backward*, this genteel romantic produced what was to become an American manifesto for social and economic reform.

Bellamy said he had no intention of writing such a book. In fact, prior to the publication of *Looking Backward*, he confessed to having no real affiliations with any of the country's existing reform movements.

"I never, previous to the publication of the work, had any affiliations with any class or sect of industrial or social reformers, nor, to make my confession complete, any particular sympathy with the undertakings of the sort," he said.

Still, *Looking Backward* became a Bible for America's populists, and Bellamy himself a national and international icon of reform.

Looking Backward was a best-seller from the first day of its publication. The first edition was published by the Boston-based Ticknor and Company in January 1888. Later that year, Ticknor was bought out by another Boston publishing company, Houghton and Mifflin.

In the first year, *Looking Backward* sold sixty thousand copies and reached well over one hundred thousand copies when editions were released in England and Europe. Within a decade, it sold more than one million copies. It has been translated into every major language, and its appeal extended far into the twentieth century, with a publication of one hundred thousand copies in 1945.

Clubs dedicated to furthering Bellamy's utopian ideas sprang up all over the country. At one point, there were close to two hundred "Bellamy" or "Nationalist" clubs. Carried along by the popularity of the book, Bellamy devoted all his time to lecturing and publicizing the ideas in the book. He edited *The New Nation*, the Nationalist movement's publication, and helped to organize the People's party in Massachusetts. Bellamy saw the Populist movement as a means of achieving lasting social change.

The country had been ready for a book like *Looking Backward* for a long time. America had been ravaged by widespread economic panics and depressions, and confrontations between workers and bosses had became more frequent and more violent. The people of America wanted a change, and Bellamy's book offered them a blueprint for a new and better world.

Looking Backward is set in the year 2000 in Boston. Julian West, the main character and narrator, was put into a hypnotic sleep in the year 1887, and through a series of circumstances does not wake up until the year 2000. There, the retired physician Dr. Leete discovers West and revives him. In conversations with Leete and his daughter Edith, West learns of all the marvelous social and economic changes that occurred during his 113-year slumber.

In the year 2000, all of American society is classless. There are no social or economic disparities. Men and women are equal. Crime has vanished. Peace and prosperity reign. All of this has been accomplished under a new "socialist" system. Under this new system, every citizen from the age twenty-one to forty-five works for the government in a national industrial army. Workers share equally in the fruits of their collective labor.

This new "socialist" world of the year 2000 that Bellamy envisioned did not come about because of violence or strikes, but through a natural collective movement to free the country of want. In the book, Bellamy compares the inadequacies of the American capitalist system of 1887 to the nationalist world of the year 2000.

In one section of the book, Julian West explains to Dr.

Leete what the role of government was during the nineteenth century.

"... the proper functions of government, strictly speaking, were limited to keeping the peace and defending the people against the public enemy...." West explains.

Dr. Leete responds, "And in heaven's name, who are the public enemies? Are they France, England, Germany, or hunger, cold and nakedness?"

Although Americans had long been suspicious of the concept of "socialism" because it conjured up an image of ruthless radicalism, Bellamy's unique form of American socialism, without violence and with its emphasis on practical and prosperous change, readily appealed to the American ideal. Making the idea of socialism palatable to American society was in and of itself a great achievement for Bellamy. *Looking Backward* introduced American society to the issue of utopian debate that lasted well into the next century. Across the country, preachers used the book as part of their sermons. Social reformers and politicians tried to find ways to turn Bellamy's ideas into reality. The entire country was swept up in this dramatic call for sweeping reform.

Through it all, Bellamy held fast to his claim that he had no intention of writing such a book. "In undertaking to write *Looking Backward*, I had, at the outset, no idea of attempting a serious contribution to the movement of social reform. The idea was of a mere literary fantasy...." he said.

Despite the success of the book and the flurry of reform activity throughout the country, both the Nationalist cause and the Populist movement floundered following the Panic of 1893, during which unemployment climbed to 2.5 million and the banking industry teetered on the brink of collapse.

Bellamy ultimately returned home to Chicopee Falls to

work on a sequel to *Looking Backward*. The book was intended to give a detailed economic rationale for the ideas expressed in *Looking Backward*. The book, *Equality*, was published nine years later, shortly before Bellamy's death. Weakened by tuberculosis, Bellamy traveled to Colorado in the hopes of recovering his strength. He died in 1898 at the age of forty-eight in Chicopee Falls.

The mere "literary fantasy" he intended to write with *Looking Backward* swept America along in a storm of social reform, and many of the long-term social and economic advances made in America in later years came from the writings of reformers like Edward Bellamy, the genteel romantic turned reformer.

24 Andrew Carnegie (1835–1919)
The Gospel of Wealth, 1889

"The best means of benefitting the community is to place within its reach the ladders upon which the aspiring can rise."

THE TIMES: Mark Twain published *A Connecticut Yankee in King Arthur's Court*. Thomas Edison and George Eastman combined their talents to produce the first movie film. The first electric sewing machine was introduced. Nellie Bly, a New York reporter, made it around the world in a record seventy-two days. The Sherman Antitrust Act was passed by Congress, and the population of America was nearly 63 million people.

The aim of most writers is to make money from the sale of their books, but Andrew Carnegie's book advocated giving money away!

Carnegie's book *The Gospel of Wealth*, published in 1900, advanced the notion that along with the freedom and benefits of great wealth came an obligation. According to Carnegie, wealthy Americans ought to use their fortunes for social good. Although he adamantly maintained the right of individuals to amass huge fortunes, he argued that they should be used for the overall betterment of mankind.

His philosophy was not merely idle chatter. He practiced what he preached, and as one of the richest men in America, he devoted the latter part of his life to distributing much of his fortune in ways that directly benefited society.

"It's a disgrace to die rich," he said.

Carnegie's book, which quickly became a best-seller, is the basis of the philanthropic movement in America.

"If I had not gone into business, I would have become a journalist," he claimed. But Carnegie did go into business, and his estimated fortune by 1900 was nearly $400 million.

Carnegie used most of his money to build libraries and endow foundations throughout America, many of which are permanent fixtures in today's society. He also gave considerable amounts of money to scientific research, including a fifty-thousand-dollar grant to Madame Curie for her research on radium. He built parks throughout the country, claiming it was his intent to bring ". . . more sweetness and light into the monotonous lives of the toiling masses." His contributions have had a far-reaching and lasting impact on American society, and through his book Carnegie was able to establish the guiding principles for the rest of America's wealthiest citizens. Carnegie often said he worked only six months out of the year. This, he claimed, allowed him time to pursue his philanthropic interests. Those who labored for him, however, were not afforded this luxury.

Carnegie, one of the richest men in America, came from humble beginnings. He was born in Scotland in a two-room cottage. He had no formal education and used his intuitive business acumen to build his fortune.

When he was a teenager, his annual earnings were ninety dollars, but by the time he was thirty years old, he was earning the unheard-of sum of fifty thousand dollars a year. Even then,

Carnegie had a theory about the money he earned beyond the fifty thousand dollars.

"Spend the surplus each year for benevolent purposes, especially those connected with education and the improvement of the poorer classes," he wrote.

The Gospel of Wealth was based on an essay entitled "Wealth," which originally appeared in 1889 in the small literary journal *The North American Review*. Although the *Review* had a limited circulation, Carnegie's far-reaching philosophy soon became the topic of discussion in both America and England. Magazines and newspapers throughout the country were soon printing excerpts of the article, while national editorials were applauding Carnegie's generous philosophy.

"The problem of our age is the proper administration of wealth, that the ties of brotherhood may still bind together the rich and the poor in harmonious relationship," he wrote.

Carnegie made his fortune in railroads and in steel. In 1901, he sold his interest in the Carnegie Steel Company to American industrialist J. P. Morgan in one of the biggest business deals in American history. Carnegie received $225 million in bonds from Morgan in the newly formed U.S. Steel Company.

After disposing of his interest in the steel company, Carnegie set about distributing his accumulated fortune in an organized and systematic way — much the same way he set about acquiring his wealth.

"It's going to be a much harder job than amassing it," he said.

Carnegie began first by creating a pension fund for employees. He also established a pension fund for retired college professors.

He helped build public libraries throughout the country, with the strict stipulation that the communities where he built the libraries agreed to maintain them. He founded the Carnegie Institute of Technology at Carnegie-Mellon University in Pittsburgh. He contributed to colleges and universities, including Tuskegee Institute, which was founded by black educator Booker T. Washington (1856–1915).

He financed the Temple of Peace at The Hague in the Netherlands and a Pan-American Palace in Washington, D.C. The list of his generous philanthropic contributions were vast and numerous — all intended to enrich the lives of every American.

Andrew Carnegie was born in Dunfermline, Scotland, in November 1835. He emigrated with his family to America in 1848 and settled in Allegheny, Pennsylvania. His family was too poor to provide him with a formal education, so he went to work in a factory where he earned little more than a dollar a week. He studied telegraphy and went to work as a telegraphy operator for the Pennsylvania Railroad, where he rose quickly through the ranks based on his brains and daring. He supplemented his meager income by investing.

He became interested in the Pullman railroad sleeper car and introduced its use into the Pennsylvania Railroad. Carnegie held a one-eighth interest in the Pullman Car Company, and this investment made him rich. His involvement with Pullman became the foundation of his growing fortune.

He invested in steel manufacturing and formed his own company to build steel railroads, bridges, buildings, and ships. By 1881, Carnegie became the leading figure in the American steel-manufacturing industry. Even in this leadership role, he spent only half his time involved in work. He did not take up his time with the day-to-day operations of his steel company, but left that in the hands of others. He worked setting policy and providing needed capital.

He was a genius at finding qualified people to work for him.

"The man isn't worth his salt who cannot have his affairs so efficiently organized that he can drop them at a moment's notice," Carnegie said.

Carnegie spent a great deal of time vacationing in his native Scotland. The rest of his time he spent educating himself, writing, and lecturing. Throughout his life, he remained acutely aware of the plight of the workers during this period of American industrialization. His book *The Gospel of Wealth* clearly defended the acquisition of great wealth, as long as that wealth was put to good use.

"The laws of accumulation will be left free, the laws of distribution free. Individualism will continue, but the millionaire will be but a trustee for the poor, intrusted . . . with a great part of the increased wealth of the community, but administering it for the community. . . ." he wrote.

Carnegie died at the age of eighty-four in August 1919 in Lenox, Massachusetts.

25 Jacob Riis (1849–1914)
How the Other Half Lives, 1890

"The most useful citizen in New York."

THE TIMES: The U.S. Weather Bureau was started. Sitting Bull, the legendary chief of the Sioux Indians, who was credited with killing George Armstrong Custer at the battle of the Little Big Horn, was killed by army troops. Emily Dickinson's first book of collected poems was published posthumously. The children's story *Black Beauty*, written by Anna Sewell, was published in America. It was estimated that only one percent of the American population controlled most of the wealth in the country.

Jacob Riis, a former carpenter, was the foremost advocate for housing reform in America. Riis, America's first reform-minded photojournalist, wrote a startling, landmark book on the condition of New York City slums, *How the Other Half Lives*. The book led to the passage of legislation to clean up the city's worst tenement districts.

How the Other Half Lives, published in 1890, brought American readers a vivid and gruesome look at some of New

York's worst slums. Many of the city's leading citizens, among them police commissioner Theodore Roosevelt, sought to end the vicious cycle of poverty in the tenement dwellings, first through legislation and later by tearing down some of the worst slums.

Riis accomplished this with words and pictures. Although photography equipment was still awkward and unsophisticated, the development of a new camera flash let Riis take a series of vivid and detailed photographs of the New York slums. With photos, line drawings, and graphic text, Riis portrayed to America the seedy underbelly of tenement living. It was perhaps Riis's emphasis on the plight of the children that most enraged affluent New Yorkers, leading them to call for the passage of reform legislation.

"Here in this tenement . . . 14 persons died that year, and 11 of them were children . . . eight of them not yet five years old. . . . There were five baby funerals in that house the same year. . . ." Riis wrote.

One of New York's worst slums, Mulberry Bend, was torn down, and a park was built in its place. Riis had a special place in his heart for children, and in 1891 published a follow-up book to *How the Other Half Lives* called *Children of the Poor*. This book exposed the plight of children living in the tenement district. Through his efforts, a settlement house providing health care and food was established to help the impoverished tenement dwellers. The settlement house was later named the Jacob Riis Settlement, in honor of the author.

Riis carried his camera equipment throughout the slums, shooting his own pictures of the decadent tenements and alleys. It was estimated that there were more than one million people squeezed into New York's wretched Lower East Side at the time. What Riis captured in his photographs (some appeared as line drawings in the book) and his text was the naked horror of disease, crime, filth, and degradation.

"In scores of back alleys, of stable lanes and hidden byways, of which the rent collector alone can keep track, they share such shelter as the ramshackle structures afford with every kind of abomination rifled from the dumps and ash barrels of the city," he wrote.

How the Other Half Lives was an immediate best-seller — a landmark in American documentary journalism. The book caught the attention of Theodore Roosevelt, then serving as the New York City police commissioner, who contacted Riis.

"I have read your book," Roosevelt told Riis. "And I have come to help."

Armed with Riis's scathing exposé, New York civic leaders began an unrelenting crusade to rid the slums of crime and degradation. Riis became known as the Great Emancipator of the Slums. He worked for the establishment of public kindergartens, vocational education, city parks and playgrounds, and a complete upheaval in tenement housing conditions — police-station lodging houses for the homeless were abolished, tenement firetraps were destroyed, and the filth and disease that afflicted the children of the slums was held in check.

Riis's view was that improving the conditions of urban life required drastic environmental changes, and so blighted buildings and firetraps were torn down, and social-welfare, education, and health-care programs were developed. He felt that the city's poor needed a chance, not simply a change.

Riis was not without his enemies — greedy landlords, corrupt politicians, and crime figures who thrived in the slums all conspired against the reform movement started by Riis. But Riis was tireless in his struggle. He often spent his own money to help the downtrodden.

Roosevelt called him "the most useful citizen in New York."

Riis confessed that he didn't know why the book enjoyed so much success or why it had the impact it had on the New York citizenry. "For myself I have never been able to explain the great run the book had. . . . Perhaps it was that I had it in me so long that it burst out with a rush that caught on. . . ." Riis said.

After the publication of *How the Other Half Lives*, Riis became the leading expert on America's urban poor and spent the next few years writing and lecturing throughout the country on the plight of the cities and its poorest inhabitants. He traveled to England and Denmark, where he studied the social-welfare programs of those countries.

In 1891, he wrote an article about the contaminated water supply in New York City that prompted state officials to prohibit the dumping of sewage into New York's reservoir. Because of the article, New York health officials were able to avert a cholera epidemic.

In 1899, when Theodore Roosevelt became governor of New York, he appointed Riis as his adviser on urban affairs. Through his efforts, hundreds of New York City tenement sweatshops were condemned, and a State Tenement Housing Commission was formed. When Roosevelt became president in 1901, Riis continued to serve as an adviser. From 1905 to 1909, he invested his energies in establishing both the Boys Club and Boy Scouts of America.

Jacob Riis was born in Denmark in 1849. He did not become an American citizen until 1885.

After serving as a carpenter's apprentice for three years, he joined the Danish carpenters' union in 1868. In 1870, he emigrated to America to find work. He held a series of odd jobs, among them coal miner, farmer, and laborer. He lived on the brink of poverty during his early years in America, and on more than one occasion landed in jail for vagrancy.

In 1874, after taking a course in telegraphy, he landed a position as a reporter for the *New York News Association*. Later he became a reporter for the *South Brooklyn News*, and worked his way up to editor. In 1875, he bought the paper and turned it into one of the city's most reform-minded publications. After selling the paper in 1877, he took a job with the *New York Tribune*, and for the next eleven years he worked as a police reporter. His stories portrayed the crowded, unsanitary conditions of the slums, and he became New York's most vocal critic.

Jacob Riis, the carpenter from Denmark, saw in America a chance to build a better world, and he devoted his life to that crusade.

He died in 1914 at the age of sixty-five, and is buried in the cemetery next to his farm in Barre, Massachusetts.

Alfred Mahan (1840–1914)

26 The Influence of Sea Power upon History, 1890

"Whoever rules the waves, rules the world."

THE TIMES: The first electrocution was held in a New York State prison. Walt Whitman published his last collection of poetry, *Goodbye, My Fancy*. Ambrose Bierce's short story "An Occurrence at Owl Creek Bridge" was published for the first time in Bierce's book *Tales*. The two-step was the most popular dance in the country, and John Philip Sousa's "Washington Post March" was the most popular song in the country.

Alfred Mahan hoped, when he published his book *The Influence of Sea Power upon History* in 1890, that America would build a navy strong enough to ensure peace around the world. Instead, some contend, it led to World War I.

Mahan's book is credited with shaping today's modern navies throughout the world. Every world power was immediately influenced by Mahan's book except for one — America. Ultimately, America too followed suit and established a powerful naval presence, but by the time it did, both Germany and Japan had already created enormous fleets.

The book was based on a series of lectures Mahan developed in 1886 while serving as a naval-history professor at the Naval War College in Newport, Rhode Island. Although it was primarily a history of Britain's sea power, Mahan wrote a compelling argument in favor of building larger naval forces. He maintained that any country wishing to attain the status of a world power had to establish a strong naval presence. According to Mahan, a sea blockade was historically more decisive than a well-armed land battle.

Mahan also maintained that true naval superiority included not only a military fleet, but a strong merchant marine and worldwide bases to ensure trade throughout the world. He argued convincingly that a flourishing merchant-marine fleet would increase trade and wealth. He also argued that safe foreign bases, protected by a strong military fleet, would ensure continued world trade.

At the time Mahan's book was published, America's navy was made up of a ragtag assortment of ships. The best of the American fleet was made up of three cruisers. It wasn't until 1889 that the first modern American battleship was built. It had no merchant-marine fleet or overseas bases and did not engage to any large degree in world trade.

Mahan argued that if America wanted to assume its rightful place as a world power, a strong naval presence was essential.

"Within, the home market is secured, but outside, beyond the broad seas, there are the markets of the world," Mahan wrote.

To further America's dominant place in the world, Mahan advocated the building of the Panama Canal as a way of opening up trade routes to world markets.

". . . it is evident enough that this canal, by modifying the direction of trade routes, will induce a great increase of commercial activity. . . . Every position in that sea will have enhanced commercial and military value, and the canal itself will become a strategic center of the most vital importance," Mahan wrote.

Mahan also called for America to annex Hawaii as a strategic commercial and military base.

President Theodore Roosevelt and U.S. senator Henry Cabot Lodge became advocates of Mahan's call for a more powerful navy. Both Roosevelt and Lodge used Mahan's arguments in their quest to expand and modernize the U.S. naval fleet. Still, America's response to Mahan's book was slow in coming compared to the rest of the world's.

In England, the book was hailed as "the gospel of England's greatness." It was used to justify Britain's naval buildup. Although Britain once ruled the waves, its navy had fallen into disrepair. Both France and Italy had far more sophisticated fleets. Because of Mahan's book, the expansion of Britain's navy was hastened by several years. Both Oxford and Cambridge universities bestowed honorary degrees on Mahan for his contributions to the strengthening of the British Navy.

In Germany, Kaiser Wilhelm II ordered copies of Mahan's book placed in the libraries onboard all German battleships. German naval officers were required to read and study Mahan's work. "It [the book] is onboard all my ships. . . . Our future lies upon the water. . . ." Wilhelm said.

In Japan, Mahan became a hero. More copies of his book were published in Japan than in any other country where the book was translated. Every Japanese warship had a copy of Mahan's book onboard. Based on his book, the Japanese built the largest naval fleet in the Orient. The Japanese government went so far as to offer Mahan a position as naval adviser for the entire feet, but Mahan declined.

In later life, Mahan, who had emphasized naval power as a means of world trade, blamed himself for Germany's naval might during the First World War. Although Mahan's book did not contribute directly to the war, he saw his words used for the purpose of expanding German's naval war effort.

Mahan's philosophy that "Whoever rules the waves, rules the world" was held by world powers until the advent of air power. During World War II, although navies still played a strategic role, it was air supremacy that was the deciding factor in most of the Pacific theater battles.

Mahan saw much of what he advocated come to pass in his lifetime. The buildup of the American Navy, the Panama Canal, and even the establishment of bases in Hawaii all occurred.

Alfred Mahan was born in 1840 in West Point, New York. His father was a professor at the U.S. Military Academy.

He graduated from the Naval Academy in 1859. During this active naval career, he never rose higher in rank than captain. It was only after his retirement that he was promoted to rear admiral — mostly because of the popularity of his book.

Mahan was fifty years old when he began his career as a lecturer at the Naval War College in Newport. Following the success of *The Influence of Sea Power upon History*, he devoted most of his time to writing and went on to produce more than twenty-one books in his lifetime.

He died at the age of seventy-four in 1914 in Washington, D.C.

27

Susan B. Anthony (1820–1906)
History of Woman Suffrage, 1881–1902

"I do not want praise. I want justice."

THE TIMES: James Naismith invented the game of basketball in Springfield, Massachusetts. Ellis Island in New York became the landing point for more than 20 million immigrants. Grover Cleveland was elected president. The final edition of Walt Whitman's *Leaves of Grass* was published. "After the Ball Is Over" was the most popular song in the country. Gentleman Jim Corbett won the world heavyweight boxing championship by knocking out John L. Sullivan in a bout that lasted twenty-one rounds.

People are free to vote as they wish in America, but voting nearly cost Susan B. Anthony her freedom! There are many people whose writing helped shape America. For some, their actions spoke louder than words. Anthony was one such person.

Born in Adams, Massachusetts, in 1820 into a Quaker family, Anthony began her career as a schoolteacher at fifteen years old. Although in later life she collaborated on the four-volume book *History of Woman Suffrage* (1881–1902), which is an incisive history of the women's movement, it was through her lifelong devotion to the cause of women's rights that she helped shape the world we now live in.

Because of her heroic actions, the Nineteenth Amendment to the U.S. Constitution was adopted in 1920. Often called the Susan B. Anthony Amendment, it gave women in America the right to vote. It was not enacted until fourteen years after her death.

It was Anthony's stirring words, delivered at her controversial trial in June 1873, that propelled the women's rights movement into the forefront of American debate. Her trial was one of the foremost political shams in American history.

Anthony began her career in the reform movement of America by becoming active in both the temperance (antidrinking) and antislavery movements. Her interest in the women's rights movement was piqued by the Seneca Falls Convention held in 1848. Out of this first organized women's convention came the Declaration of Women's Rights, which demanded free education, equal opportunity, free speech, and the right to vote. In part, the convention and Declaration were founded on the principles set forth by Margaret Fuller (1810–50) in her landmark work *Woman in the Nineteenth Century*. Although inspired by the convention, Anthony did not begin her work on behalf of women's rights in earnest until five years later.

In 1853, she gave her first speech on behalf of women's rights at the New York Teachers' Association. Anthony became the first woman to speak before the assembled group — despite the fact that two thirds of its membership were women.

Anthony's first victory on behalf of women came at this meeting when the New York State Teacher's Association adopted a measure that recognized the rights of women teachers to "share in all the privileges and deliberations of this body."

During the Civil War, Anthony was active in the organization of the Woman's National Loyal League, which supported the Union cause and advocated the emancipation of slaves and equal rights for women. When the war ended, Anthony worked tirelessly on behalf of the cause of women's rights.

". . . another form of slavery remains to be disposed of," she said, talking about the need for the emancipation of women.

As her reputation as an outspoken and articulate advocate of the women's rights movement grew, so did the attacks upon her. Cartoons appeared in newspapers across the country depicting her as a half-naked cigar-chomping harpy who advocated free love and other unnatural vices. "Such heresies would make demons of the pit shudder. . . ." a *Syracuse Star* editorial declared. But Anthony would not be discouraged. She traveled the country organizing women's groups and lecturing. Her tireless crusade on behalf of women's rights earned her the title of "the Napoleon of the Feminist Movement."

In New York, she submitted an amendment guaranteeing rights for women. For six years, she submitted the amendment to New York legislators, and every year it was rejected. Finally, in 1860, on her seventh attempt, the legislature adopted her amendment.

In the 1872 presidential election, Anthony organized a group of women to register and vote at the Rochester, New York, polls. Since it was illegal for women to vote in America, Anthony was arrested.

Anthony pleaded not guilty to the charges. She argued that women had been given the right to vote under the Fourteenth Amendment of the Constitution, which gave black Americans the right to vote. The amendment gave every American citizen the right to vote and defined a citizen as any person born or naturalized in America. Anthony claimed that the Fourteenth Amendment made no mention of sex; therefore, all American women who were citizens of the United States had the right to vote.

President Grant, who oversaw one of the most corrupt administrations in the country's history, stacked the deck against Anthony. He appointed one of his many political hacks, Ward Hunt, to preside over Anthony's trial. Hunt was an associate justice of the Supreme Court at the time, and it was unheard of for the Supreme Court to involve itself in a lower-court trial.

Anthony's trial lasted a mere two days. In the course of the trial, she was called to testify in her own defense, but Judge Hunt refused to let her take the stand, saying Anthony was a woman and therefore not competent to testify in a court of law. After all the evidence had been presented to the jury, Judge Hunt ordered the jury to find Anthony guilty. The jury was speechless, and the spectators in the courtroom shocked. Despite the protests by Anthony's lawyer, Hunt told the stunned jury, "you say you find the defendant guilty of the offense . . . so say you all." There was no deliberation by the jury. Hunt found Anthony guilty, and sentencing was scheduled for the next day. She faced a possible five-hundred-dollar fine and three years in prison.

At the trial the next day, Hunt allowed Anthony to say a few words before he passed sentence. As soon as Anthony began to speak, Judge Hunt realized the blunder he had made. All eyes were glued to Anthony as she gave her impassioned speech. Every word of it was recorded by reporters in the courtroom. The next day, her eloquent words were spread across the front pages of most of the country's leading newspapers.

To Judge Hunt, she said, "You have trampled underfoot every vital principle of our government. My natural rights, my civil rights, my political rights are all ignored."

Hunt tried to silence her by pounding his gavel and proclaiming, "You've been tried according to established forms of law."

". . . by forms of law made by men, interpreted by men, administered by men, in favor of men — and against women," Anthony said.

Hunt sentenced her to a fine of one hundred dollars, which Anthony swore she'd never pay, and she never did.

Although her trial awakened the collective consciousness of the nation, real change was slow in coming. Anthony spent the rest of her life organizing and lecturing on women's rights, and became internationally famous.

"I do not want praise. I want justice," she said.

Anthony did not live to see the day when women could vote. She died in Rochester, New York, shortly after her eighty-sixth birthday.

At her last public appearance, held shortly before her death, Anthony echoed her final plea on behalf of women's rights.

"Failure," she proclaimed, "is impossible."

28 Stephen Crane (1871–1900)
Maggie: A Girl of the Streets, 1893

"Environment is a tremendous thing in the world."

THE TIMES: The workers at the Carnegie Steel Company went on strike. Violence erupted when Andrew Carnegie called in more than three hundred Pinkerton agents to break up the strike. Ten strikers were killed. The first gas-powered car was built by Charles and Frank Duryea. In Fall River, Massachusetts, Lizzie Borden was accused of killing her father and stepmother with an ax. *The Strange Case of Doctor Jekyll and Mr. Hyde* by Robert Louis Stevenson was published in America. The zipper was invented.

Stephen Crane, who many American critics claimed was the father of modern American fiction, could not sell his first book, *Maggie: A Girl of the Streets*, to any publisher, because it was deemed too brutal. According to Crane, he wrote the book while he was still in college. "I wrote it in two days, before Christmas," he said.

The publishers he submitted it to called it brutal, shocking, and profane. Using the money he borrowed from his brother,

Crane published the book himself in 1893. It was bound in a cheap paperback cover bearing the pseudonym "Johnson Smith." It never sold a single copy and ended up languishing in Crane's room, where he kept the copies stored. He was only twenty-one years old when he published the book.

Maggie is the story of a beautiful girl living in the New York slums who endures abject poverty and degradation at the hands of an alcoholic mother and an indifferent boyfriend. She ultimately drowns herself. The novel was short, filled with violent episodes and blunt language.

". . . they entered into a dark region where, from a careening building, a dozen gruesome doorways gave up loads of babies to the street and gutter. . . . The building quivered and creaked from the weight of humanity stamping about in its bowels," Crane wrote.

His view of the violence and degradation of the New York slums appalled every publisher who initially read the book. According to Crane, he wanted to demonstrate that "environment is a tremendous thing in the world. . . ."

Crane was not a crusader for social reform. His book was not an indictment of the conditions of New York's slums, but a genuine depiction of those conditions and its impact on society. Crane believed that it was impossible to hide behind the social veneers of the times and still produce worthwhile art.

"We are most successful in art when we approach nearest to nature and truth," he declared.

In *Maggie*, Crane depicted a world where even goodness and beauty would succumb to the violence of an unchecked environment.

"The girl, Maggie, blossomed in a mud puddle. She grew to be a most rare and wonderful production of a tenement district, a pretty girl," he wrote.

Crane based the book on his own firsthand experiences living on New York's Bowery. After attending and dropping out of Lafayette College and Syracuse University, Crane went to New York City in 1890 to live and work as a newspaper reporter. According to Crane, he moved to the slums of New York in order to experience "all the sensations of life."

Although *Maggie* never sold a copy, it impressed several leading literary figures of the times, who hailed Crane's work as pioneering in the world of literary fiction.

His next book, *The Red Badge of Courage*, was published in 1895. Unlike *Maggie*, which was written from Crane's own real-life experiences, *The Red Badge of Courage* was written entirely from his fertile imagination. Crane claimed he wrote it in a matter of ten days.

The Red Badge of Courage is a story about an anonymous Civil War battle and the struggle of the main character with his tormenting conflict between courage and fear. At the time Crane wrote it, he had never even been near a battlefield. The entire book was based on research he had done and brought imaginatively to life in his fiction.

Although Crane had no military experience when he wrote it, *The Red Badge of Courage* was hailed, even by Civil War veterans, as an authentic depiction of a soldier's feelings during battle.

The book was first published in serial form in December 1894 in the *Philadelphia Press*. It was a condensed version of eighteen thousand words; the manuscript was fifty thousand words in its original form. Following its initial publication, *The Red Badge of Courage* appeared in its entirety in early December in the *New York Press*. The story was so well received that it ultimately appeared in newspapers throughout the country.

It was published in book form in 1895 and became a best-seller both in America and England. It went through nine editions within the first year, and Crane was hailed as the author of a classic war novel.

The original publication had netted Crane a mere hundred dollars, but the novel went on to become his most financially successful book.

Responding to the criticism that he had never seen any military action, Crane proposed to his critics that any good writer should be able to "say something worthwhile about any event."

Following the success of *The Red Badge of Courage*, Crane was hailed both in America and England as one of the country's most gifted writers. He was only twenty-two years old at the time, but his career and life were short. In 1896, his first novel, *Maggie*, was republished, and although it was reviewed favorably by critics, it did not sell well. His poems were published in 1895 under the title *The Black Riders*.

At the outbreak of the Spanish-American War, Crane served as a correspondent for the *New York World* in Cuba, where he was cited for bravery under fire. His later work consisted mostly of short stories, most notable among them "The Open Boat," "The Blue Hotel," and "The Bride Comes to Yellow Sky." English author H. G. Wells hailed Crane's "The Open Boat" as the greatest short story ever written.

Stephen Crane, who was born in Newark, New Jersey, in 1871, became an author of international fame by the time he was twenty-five years old.

He left America to live in England, commenting, "You can have an idea in England without being sent to jail for it."

He died in Germany at the age of twenty-nine while trying to recover from tuberculosis.

Henry Demarest Lloyd
(1847–1903)
29 *Wealth Against Commonwealth,* 1894

"Independent in everything, neutral in nothing."

THE TIMES: Over one million bicycles were recorded in use in America. Coxey's Army, a band of unemployed workers, marched on Washington, D.C. "The Sidewalks of New York" was the most popular song in the country. The Pullman railroad-car strike began. *The Prisoner of Zenda* by Anthony Hope was published along with Rudyard Kipling's anthology of children's stories, *The Jungle Book*. One of the most popular books in the country was *Beautiful Joe*, a dog story, written by Margaret Marshall Saunders. The book sold nearly one million copies.

Henry Demarest Lloyd's book *Wealth Against Commonwealth*, published in 1894, didn't produce any of the changes the author thought it would, but it *did* usher in a new form of journalism that ultimately helped shape America!

Lloyd's book began as an article that appeared in the Boston, Massachusetts-based magazine *Atlantic Monthly*. The article, called "The Story of a Great Monopoly," appeared in the magazine in March 1881. It depicted the unethical tactics used by the Standard Oil Company to eliminate competition. Lloyd's article ushered in a new era in literature — "the literature of exposure" — which later became known throughout the country as "muckraking." The article served as the prototype for this new type of journalism.

The *Atlantic Monthly* article became the basis for Lloyd's book *Wealth Against Commonwealth*, published in 1894. Lloyd wrote the nearly five-hundred-page book based on court records and the findings of congressional committees. In it, he brought to the public's attention the unethical practices of monopolies in America, specifically the Standard Oil Company, exposing the abuse of power in their quest for money.

Although the book was widely read, it did not produce any immediate changes in the way America's business was conducted. But it did accomplish two important things. It paved the way for other writers, creating a whole new genre of writing in the country — muckraking journalism — and it demonstrated that in the right hands congressional records and court documents could be transformed into highly readable literature.

Lloyd warned readers against the rising power of monopolies in America, demonstrating the abuse of such institutions as government, laws, and churches by monopolies, solely for the purpose of acquiring vast wealth. Lloyd maintained that America's future depended on cooperation between business and labor working for the social and economic well-being of everyone.

Wealth Against Commonwealth was not Lloyd's first venture into literature aimed at exposing abuses in business. His first book, *A Strike of Millionaires Against Miners*, published in 1890, was an impassioned plea for industrial justice based on the Spring Valley coal strike in which mine owners used the laws to oppress coal miners.

In 1893, Lloyd worked as an organizer for the Milwaukee streetcar workers, and in 1894 he defended the Socialist union organizer, Eugene Debs, against charges stemming from the Pullman railroad strike. Lloyd, who had no sympathy for violence or radical tactics, defended the cause of the anarchists involved in the Haymarket Massacre of 1886. His efforts led to the commutation of the death sentence against two convicted Haymarket anarchists. He also wrote articles defending the interest of organized labor and small businessmen, and advocated for the eight-hour workday.

Born in New York City in 1847, Henry Demarest Lloyd attended Columbia College Law School and was admitted to the New York bar in 1869. He was active in the Young Men's Municipal Reform Association in New York, which helped drive the corrupt Boss Tweed crowd from political office.

In 1873, Lloyd moved to Chicago, where he served for thirteen years as a financial editor and writer for the *Chicago Tribune*. In 1885, he resigned and became the leading reform writer of his times. In 1894, he ran for Congress, as a National People's party candidate, but was defeated.

From 1897 to 1901, he traveled throughout Europe and New Zealand studying labor relations and social conditions. In 1900, he published *A Country Without Strikes*, based on New Zealand's compulsory labor arbitration, but the book did not influence either business or labor in America.

In 1903, shortly before his death at the age of fifty-six, Lloyd was engaged in a campaign for municipal ownership of the streetcar system in Chicago.

Throughout his life, *Wealth Against Commonwealth* remained his most widely read book. He died in Chicago in 1903.

30
Fannie Farmer (1857–1915)
The Boston Cooking-School Cook Book, 1896

"Good judgement, with experience, has taught some to measure by sight, but the majority need definite guides."

THE TIMES: "America the Beautiful," written by Katherine Lee Bates, was published for the first time. William McKinley was elected president. The first comic strip, "The Yellow Kid," was published in the *New York World*. The novel *Quo Vadis?* by Henryk Sienkiewicz was published. Edward Arlington Robinson's first book of poetry, *The Torrent and the Night Before*, was published. The first moving pictures were shown at a New York music hall. The first Ford automobile rolled off the assembly line, and gold was discovered in the Klondike.

Fannie Farmer's *Boston Cooking-School Cook Book*, published in 1896, had all the ingredients for a best-seller, but her publisher didn't want to take any chances and demanded that Farmer pay for the production of the first edition.

The publisher, Little, Brown and Company of Boston, was afraid that her new recipes wouldn't catch on with the reading public. The publisher wasn't even sure there was a "reading public" for the book. At the time it was published in 1896, cookbooks fell into two categories. The first were slapdash recipes aimed at stretching the household budget. These were targeted for large poor families. The second type of cookbook was aimed specifically at household chefs, who had at their disposal all the cooking supplies and implements that you might find in a London or Paris restaurant. Fannie Farmer's cookbook was neither of these.

Farmer's intent was to provide middle-class working families with a basic but comprehensive book on good cooking. It included recipes and menus, and was a step-by-step guide that was so easy to use that anyone who could follow its simple instructions could easily prepare a nutritious meal. It was so comprehensive that it even offered tips on how to ignite the right fire, depending on the fuel you were using (wood, coal, etc.).

Until the publication of Farmer's book, recipes were always written with vague instructions on the quantity of ingredients needed. They called for a pinch of this or a handful of that, a heaping or scant cupful, a generous teaspoon or pat of butter. Called "the Mother of Level Measurements," Farmer introduced level cooking measurements, which made recipes more accurate.

Her recipes popularized level measurement. Her instructions called for the reader to fill the cup, tablespoon, or other measuring device and then level it off by running a knife across the top of it, leaving the contents level with the rim of the utensil.

Her uniform level measurements transformed cooking into a near-exact science.

Born in Boston in March 1857, Farmer was thirty-eight years old when she wrote *The Boston Cooking-School Cook Book*. At sixteen years old, she had suffered a stroke that left one of her legs paralyzed. The paralysis prohibited her from attending college. Instead, she went to work in the household of a family friend, where she developed an interest in cooking. It was during this period that she began to collect and standardize recipes.

At twenty-eight years old, she enrolled in the Boston Cooking School, then under the direction of Carrie Dearborn. After her graduation from the school in 1889, she was appointed assistant director, and in 1891, following the death of Mrs. Dearborn, she became the director, a position she had held for eleven years when she published her cookbook.

The Boston Cooking-School Cook Book was originally privately printed by Farmer and used only with students at the Boston Cooking School. The book was finally published by Little, Brown in 1896. It subsequently went on to sell more than 4 million copies in twenty-one editions.

Brown printed only three thousand copies of the first edition, which Farmer paid for. The six-hundred-page book was priced inexpensively and quickly sold out. Over the years, it has been ranked as the sixth all-time best-seller among hardcover books in America from 1896 until the mid-1960s. For close to seventy years, it was the number-one best-selling cookbook in the country.

Following the enormous success of the book, Farmer resigned her position at the Boston Cooking School (1902) and began her own cooking school, Miss Farmer's School of Cookery. Most American cooking schools of the period were aimed at educating teachers in the theory of cooking, but Farmer's school was established to teach practical cooking to housewives.

The school taught old-fashioned home cooking and stayed

away from fancy gourmet dishes. Farmer's school soon became as popular as her cookbook, with some classes holding up to two hundred students. Farmer became America's leading authority on cooking and was a much sought-after lecturer. For ten years, she wrote a column on cooking in the national magazine *Woman's Home Companion*.

Farmer's cooking school provided courses on cooking for invalids and held training classes for nurses. Farmer taught a weekly course at the Harvard Medical School on the topic. In 1904, she published *Food and Cookery for the Sick and Convalescent*. Altogether she published six cookbooks in her lifetime, but none ever achieved the success of her revolutionary first book.

In 1907, she suffered another stroke that left both legs paralyzed, and she was forced to lecture while seated in a wheelchair. With diet, exercise, and sheer willpower, she continued teaching, writing, and lecturing for another eight years. Farmer remained, until her death, a firm believer in the benefits of healthy diets.

"I certainly feel that the time is not far distant when a knowledge of the principles of diet will be an essential part of everyone's education. Then mankind will eat to live, will be able to do better mental and physical work, and disease will be less frequent," Farmer wrote.

Farmer was still lecturing a little more than a week before she died in Boston in January 1915 at the age of fifty-seven. Her cooking school closed in 1944.

Over the years, *The Boston Cooking-School Cook Book* has been uniformly criticized by gourmet-cooking critics and chefs as being too fundamental in its approach. *Gourmet Magazine* once noted that the book "is a good guide on the foothills but not on the mountains [of good cooking]." Even in its earliest editions, the book was panned. H. L. Mencken (1880–1956) noted that the book might improve the art of cooking in America if followed, but "not a great deal perhaps. . . ."

What Mencken and other critics didn't realize was that the fundamental ingredient Farmer put into her book was plain and simple knowledge, which everyone was truly hungry for.

31 Edwin Markham (1852–1940) "The Man with the Hoe," 1899

"The battle cry for the next thousand years."

THE TIMES: The first Boston Marathon was held. The battleship *Maine* blew up in Havana, Cuba. The Spanish-American War began. *David Harum*, a novel written by Edward Noyes Westcott, was published posthumously and went on to sell more than one million copies. A peace treaty with Spain was signed, ending the Spanish-American War. "My Wild Irish Rose" was one of the most popular songs in the country.

The poem that was once hailed as the "the battle cry for the next thousand years" is hardly remembered today!

American poet Edwin Markham, who once wrote greeting-card verses for a living, also wrote one of the most inspiring and best-known poems in American literature.

"The Man with the Hoe," first published in January 1899 in the *San Francisco Examiner* newspaper, was the single most financially successful poem ever written in America. The poem, based on the painting of the same title by the French painter Jean-François Millet, was republished in more than ten thousand newspapers and magazines during Markham's lifetime. It was translated into more than forty languages and reportedly earned Markham close to $250,000.

Markham was celebrated as America's greatest living poet. When his eightieth birthday was celebrated at Carnegie Hall in 1932, countries from around the world sent delegations, while the public schools in Staten Island, where he lived, closed in his honor. His entire career was based on this single powerful poem, and although he produced other notable works in his lifetime, nothing ever equaled the success of "The Man with the Hoe."

Markham had seen Millet's painting in 1886 at an exhibit in San Francisco. He was so taken by it that he began writing his poem shortly after viewing it. The poem languished in his notebook for several years, and it was not until his wife urged him to complete it that Markham finally finished it.

Anna Markham brought the poem to the attention of the editor of the *San Francisco Examiner*, Bailey Millard. Millard was so impressed by it that he published the poem on the front page of the paper, adorned it in ornate typeface, and added a dramatic illustration. It was only forty-nine lines long, written in blank verse, but it succeeded in capturing the mood of the nation. It captured the economic and social climate of the times so completely that it was immediately hailed as a masterpiece of American poetry.

A protest poem, "The Man with the Hoe" praised the hardworking laborer, while calling to task those who exploited him.

Markham's attack on the ruling class, those he called "masters, lords and rulers in all lands," touched off a storm of controversy. A prize of ten thousand dollars was offered by businessmen to respond to Markham's scathing attack upon them. The poem's critics called it "socialistic propaganda," while its defenders hailed it as "impressive in the highest degree."

"If its author had made no other bid for fame, this one bid would suffice," said author Jack London (1876–1916). Social critics of the day said that Markham's poem would become "the battle cry for the next thousand years." The poem became a constant source of editorial discussion. Markham admitted that writing for him usually meant arguing for social reform, but disclaimed being a socialist and maintained his status as a registered Republican.

"Nobility consists of two things — reverence for women and consecration to Social Solidarity," Markham claimed.

Despite the controversy surrounding the poem, Markham's first volume of poems, *The Man with the Hoe and Other Poems*, published in 1899, found a vast audience, even among businessmen who had initially condemned the title poem. The book contained very few reform-minded poems, aside from the title poem. Instead, it was a collection of conventional poetry on beauty, art, and love.

Although Markham's career was solidly established with the publication of "The Man with the Hoe," some of his later work also proved both successful and enlightening.

In 1890, he was commissioned by the Republican Club of New York to write a poem honoring President Lincoln's birthday. Markham wrote "Lincoln, the Man of the People," which he read before an audience at Delmonico's Restaurant in New York. The next day, the poem appeared in almost every major newspaper in the country. Markham's book *Lincoln and Other Poems* was published in 1901.

In 1922, former president William Howard Taft invited Markham to read the poem at the dedication of the Lincoln Memorial in Washington. Markham recited the poem in front of more than one hundred thousand people at the dedication. The recital was aired across the country in one of the first live radio broadcasts.

From 1906 to 1907, Markham wrote a series of articles on the abuses of children in the work force, which appeared in *Cosmopolitan* magazine. His collection of articles, along with others, were published in book form in 1914 as *The Children of Bondage*, which became a landmark book in the crusade for adequate child-labor laws in America.

From 1901 on, Markham, who became known as the unofficial poet laureate of America and the voice of progressive reform in the country, lived on Staten Island, where he continued to write.

During his lifetime, he was in constant demand as a lecturer and toured the country giving readings from his work. In 1910, he founded the Poetry Society of America, which was based on get-togethers he held at his house each weekend on Staten Island. Many of the country's leading writers and poets were often guests of Markham's.

In 1936, at the age of eighty-four, he suffered a stroke that left him bedridden. He died in 1940, and his body lay in state for two days while thousands of mourners came to pay their last respects. He is buried in Los Angeles.

Markham was born in Oregon in 1852. After his parents divorced, he moved to California with his mother. He attended Christian College, from which he graduated in 1873. He taught school and was elected county superintendent of schools in California. His earliest poems appeared in *Scribner's* and *Century Magazine*, and for a time he wrote poetry for a Boston, Massachusetts, greeting-card company.

The popularity of Markham's work led to the publication

of more poetry in America's many magazines and newspapers. It was his success with "The Man with the Hoe" that convinced publishers there was a market for poetry in America. His poetry was clearly accessible to people of all walks of life, which contributed to his lifetime popularity.

32 Theodore Dreiser (1871–1945) Sister Carrie, 1900

"Chipping it out of solid rock."

THE TIMES: A hurricane in Galveston, Texas, killed six thousand people. *The Wonderful Wizard of Oz*, written by L. Frank Baum, was published. "Stars and Stripes Forever," by John Philip Sousa, was one of the most popular tunes in the country. The U.S. Census recorded nearly 76 million people in America. Nearly eight thousand cars were registered in the country, but only ten miles of roadways were paved for automobile travel. The Eastman Kodak Company introduced the Brownie camera.

Theodore Dreiser was one of America's most patient authors. His first book, *Sister Carrie*, was published in 1900, but was suppressed by the publisher. It was another twenty-five years before Dreiser would publish his next *major* work of fiction — *An American Tragedy* — a book that would catapult him into the forefront of American literature.

Sister Carrie had an enormous impact on American literature and culture. Dreiser was working as a newspaper reporter in Toledo in 1899 when he began writing *Sister Carrie* at the urging of the playwright Arthur Henry, who was himself a former newspaper reporter. He began with only a title and an idea. Nine months later, he finished the book.

Loosely based on his own sister Emma, who had eloped with an older man, the titular heroine, Carrie Meeber, is a young girl who goes off to seek her fortune in Chicago. Carrie first moves in with a salesman, and later she becomes the lover of a wealthy middle-aged man named George Hurstwood. With each illicit relationship, Carrie's career advances. After eloping to New York City with her married lover, Hurstwood, she becomes a successful actress, while he sinks deeper into despair. Carrie finally leaves him to pursue her career, and Hurstwood commits suicide.

The book was shocking for its times, not only because Dreiser dramatized the American success story in realistic terms, offering a simmering account of urban life, but because there was no retribution for Carrie's immorality. Indeed, just the opposite occurred — Carrie is *rewarded* for her immoral behavior.

"We live in an age in which the impact of material forces is well-nigh irresistible; the spiritual nature is overwhelmed by the shock," Dreiser wrote.

By today's literary standards, *Sister Carrie* seems tame, but during the 1900s Dreiser's tale of moral deterioration was shocking and offensive — not only to the public but to the publisher as well. The book was rejected outright by the first publisher it was sent to. It was then sent to Doubleday, Page, where Frank Norris (1870–1902) was a reader. Norris, a novelist and newspaper reporter best known for his naturalistic novel *McTeague* (1899), and later the muckraking novel *The Octopus* (1901), saw in Dreiser's book the workings of a true American literary genius. At Norris's urging, Frank Doubleday, the president of the publishing house, accepted the book.

Frank Doubleday's wife managed to get her hands on *Sister Carrie*, and after reading it, convinced her husband that Dreiser's work was immoral and unfit for publication. A limited number of copies had already been published, but only as a means of complying with the legal contract the publishing house had with Dreiser. Even these few copies Doubleday virtually suppressed. Only one thousand copies of the book were printed, and fewer than half were sold. No attempt was made by Doubleday to promote the book, and the few book reviewers who did manage to get their hands on a copy gave it scathing reviews.

Doubleday agreed to publish the book only with a revised ending in which the reader is given the impression that Carrie's life of sin will ultimately be punished.

"In your rocking chair, by your window, shall you dream such happiness as you may never feel," Dreiser's revised ending reads.

The failure of the book left Dreiser's career and reputation in jeopardy. It was not until 1906 that the book was finally widely circulated, after it was published by a small publishing house.

One of Dreiser's few admirers was the author H. L. Mencken (1880–1956). Dreiser helped launch Mencken's career by recommending him in 1908 for a job as a book reviewer for the magazine *The Smart Set*. Their friendship lasted eighteen years. It ended in 1925, when Mencken gave Dreiser's novel *An American Tragedy* a scathing review (one of the few critics to do so). He called it, among other things, "a vast, sloppy thing of 385,000 words, at least 250,000 of them unnecessary."

Following the critical and financial failure of *Sister Carrie*,

Dreiser suffered a nervous breakdown that left him unable or unwilling to complete his second novel. Instead, he turned his attentions to editing. By 1910, he was one of the highest-paid editors in the country, serving as the editor in chief for three national women's magazines — *The Delineator*, *The Designer*, and *The New Idea*. These three magazines had a combined circulation of 1.2 million readers during Dreiser's stewardship. When asked how a man of his talent could waste his time editing fashion magazines, Dreiser replied, "One must live."

Dreiser was born in Terre Haute, Indiana, on August 28, 1871. He was one of thirteen children. His father was a prosperous businessman but lost his fortune in a fire that destroyed the factory he owned. Since it was not insured, the Dreiser family was left penniless.

Following the fire, the family was forced to move from town to town throughout Indiana, as the elder Dreiser sought work. Theodore found school boring and attended only one year of high school before striking out on his own, first in Chicago and later New York City.

He worked a series of jobs from washing dishes to serving as a clerk in a hardware store. When he was eighteen, he entered Indiana University, but he found college life boring. He wrote that college ". . . did not concern ordinary life at all." He left the university and became a reporter for the *Chicago Globe* newspaper in 1892 at the age of twenty-one. A series of newspaper jobs followed in Chicago, New York, Cleveland, Toledo, and Pittsburgh.

After several successful years serving as an editor, he went back to writing full time and produced a series of notable works, among them *Jennie Gerhardt*, his long-awaited second novel published in 1911; *The Financier* (1912); and *The Titan* (1914). But it was not until the publication of *An American*

Tragedy, twenty-five years after the publication of *Sister Carrie*, that he garnered the critical and financial acclaim he felt he deserved.

Based on a 1906 New York murder case, *An American Tragedy* is the story of a young man's quest to achieve the great American dream of success — at any price, including murder. In the book, Clyde Griffiths kills his pregnant girlfriend because she stands in the way of his social and financial aspirations.

The book was nearly four hundred thousand words long. Dreiser explained that writing it was like ". . . chipping it out of solid rock." Within the first two weeks of its publication, *An American Tragedy* sold more than fourteen thousand copies at an unheard-of cover price of $12.50. It was immediately hailed as a masterpiece.

At long last, Theodore Dreiser achieved his crowning glory. Still, he was not satisfied. Even during the darkest days of the *Sister Carrie* publication, Dreiser considered himself America's greatest writer. The success of *An American Tragedy*, he felt, was long overdue. Even after the critical and financial success of the book, he complained that other, less deserving writers were garnering all the major literary awards, while he went unrewarded.

He once urged his friend H. L. Mencken to nominate him for a Nobel Prize in Literature, an award he never received. Ironically, one of the writers he despised most, Sinclair Lewis (1885–1951), went on to become the first American author to win the Nobel Prize in 1930. In his Nobel acceptance speech, Lewis named Theodore Dreiser as one of the American authors whose body of work should have earned him the coveted prize.

Theodore Dreiser died in 1945 at the age of seventy-four in Hollywood, California. His novel *Sister Carrie* changed the way Americans looked at themselves, and the way American writers chose to write about the world they lived in. He left behind the realization, shocking for most Americans, that the price of success, especially in the big city, comes at the price of moral deterioration, and that this is a condition of the world.

33 Frank Norris (1870–1902)
The Octopus, 1901

"Life is not always true to life."

THE TIMES: Silk stockings became popular with American women. *Mrs. Wiggs of the Cabbage Patch*, by Alice Hegan Rice, was published. William McKinley was assassinated in Buffalo, New York. Teddy Roosevelt was sworn in as president. It was discovered that yellow fever was transmitted by mosquitoes. The first great Texas oil strike occurred near Beaumont, Texas.

Although written as a novel, *The Octopus*, published in 1901, is viewed as one of America's first great economic studies.

The story focuses on the economic struggle of wheat growers in California and their battle against the corrupt and greedy railroad industry that controlled their economic future. Although Norris brings to light the inherent evils of the man-made economic system (the railroads), the book does not openly condemn the railroads. It merely seeks to show the American reading public the evils of the system they created.

At the turn of the century, when the book was written, America was moving swiftly from being an agrarian society to an industrialized one. The country had depended on the land for its livelihood, but now it had created a means of distributing the fruits of its labor and had to face the inevitable consequences of the system.

The Octopus was the first book in a planned trilogy called *The Epic of the Wheat*, an undertaking that many critics hailed as the most ambitious trilogy of its generation. Norris, however, did not live to complete the books.

The Octopus, the first book in the planned trilogy, dealt with the struggle between the wheat farmers and the railroad industry. The second book, *The Pit*, which focused on grain speculation in the Chicago marketplace, was published posthumously in 1903. The third book, *The Wolf*, which was to focus on how the wheat was consumed by the hungry masses in Europe, was never written.

Without intending to, Norris did for the railroad industry and wheat production in America what Upton Sinclair (1878–1968) did for the Chicago meat-packing industry. He exposed the plight of American farmers at the hands of the greedy railroad industry. Publication of the book led to investigations into the railroad industry's grip on American economics.

The book was based on the true-life struggles of the California wheat farmers and the Southern Pacific Railroad. During the 1870s and 1880s, much of the farmland in the San Joaquin Valley was owned by the railroad. The land was offered to the farmers for a few dollars per acre, in the hope that the farmers would settle and improve the land.

After years of cultivating the land, the farmers offered to buy it from the railroad at the agreed-upon price. Because of the vast improvements made by the farmers, making the land much more valuable, the railroad upped the price of the land nearly one hundred times the original asking price. The wheat farmers fought back, demanding that the railroad live up to its original offer.

The battle led to bloodshed, with many farmers being driven off the land they had worked so hard to cultivate. Using corrupt politicians and their vast wealth, the railroad industry finally won out.

The title of the book came from the railroad industry's long--reaching tentacles into all aspects of California life.

The Octopus received critical praise across the country and became a best-seller, standing the test of time even to this day. The initial four thousand hardcover copies of the book sold out immediately, and a second paperback edition of eight thousand also sold out within the year.

It wasn't until the publication of *The Octopus* that Norris was able to enjoy some modest financial success. Prior to its publication, he had been living on the minimal royalties of his earlier books and the small salary he received as a reader for Doubleday, Page and Company, his own publisher. Altogether, his income came to about a hundred dollars a month. The success of *The Octopus* freed him to pursue his work unencumbered by money problems.

Norris's idea in writing the book was to demonstrate the struggle that exists between Nature (the wheat) and man-made machines (the railroad). Although there are human characters in the book, it is the wheat that remains the central character.

Although Norris clearly sympathizes with the wheat farmers, many critics faulted Norris for not attacking the railroad industry more severely. Norris maintained that his goal was not to show the evils of the railroads, but to convince readers that in the end, it is Nature, no matter what economic forces are conspiring against her, who will ultimately win out.

In the most climactic scene in the book, the villain, a spokesman for the railroads, is buried alive by the very wheat he is trying to cheat the farmers out of.

"There it was. The Wheat! The Wheat! . . . It was there, everywhere. . . ." Norris wrote.

What Norris gave the reading public was a naturalist's optimistic view of the world. What the reading public chose to see was an indictment of the railroad industry.

"Life is not always true to life," Norris said, ". . . we do not care about what life actually is, but what it looks like. . . ."

What it looked like to Norris was a world where Nature, above everything else, would overcome every obstacle.

Frank Norris was born in Chicago in March 1870. In 1884, his family moved to California and settled in San Francisco. He attended private schools, where he showed a great aptitude in art. His parents sent him to London and later Paris to study. He was ultimately accepted at the University of California in 1890 as a conditional student. Although tutored, Norris was unable to grasp mathematics, and he left the university in 1894 without obtaining a degree.

He entered Harvard University in 1895, where he studied creative writing for a year. It was at Harvard that Norris wrote his first novel, *Vandover and the Brute*, which was not published until 1914. He then wrote *McTeague*, a novel about a working-class scoundrel who escapes detection in his illegal practice of dentistry among San Francisco's poor. This book was not published until 1899.

Following his stint at Harvard, he returned to San Francisco, where he joined the staff of the *San Francisco Chronicle* and was sent to cover the Boer War in South Africa. While there, he contracted African fever and was sent home to recover.

Back in San Francisco, he took a position with the literary magazine *Wave*, where his work attracted the attention of *McClure's Magazine*.

At the outbreak of the Spanish-American War in 1898, *McClure's* sent him to Cuba as a war correspondent. While in Cuba, he met Stephen Crane (1871–1900), who was also serving as a correspondent, covering the war for a competing publication. While in Cuba, Norris again suffered a recurrence of African fever and was sent home to recover. None of Norris's reports on the Spanish-American War were published by *McClure's*.

Following his recovery, he went back to work as a low-paid reader for Doubleday, Page and Company. While working there, Norris first read the novel *Sister Carrie* by Theodore Dreiser (1871–1945). It was at Norris's insistence that Dreiser's book was ultimately published.

Norris became ill shortly after the completion of the second book in *The Epic of The Wheat* trilogy and was admitted to the hospital suffering from a fever and severe stomach cramps. He died on October 25, 1902, at the age of thirty-two.

34 W.E.B. Du Bois (1868–1963)
The Souls of Black Folk, 1903

"The Negro race, like all races, is going to be saved by exceptional men."

THE TIMES: The first motion picture, *The Great Train Robbery*, was shown. *Rebecca of Sunnybrook Farm*, written by Kate Douglas Wiggin, was published. It sold more than one million copies. Jack London published his most popular book, *The Call of the Wild*. Orville and Wilbur Wright flew the first powered airplane at Kitty Hawk, North Carolina. The first World Series in baseball was played and won by the Red Stockings (later the Boston Red Sox).

The man who did more than any other black American to further the cause of civil rights in this country during the first half of the twentieth century is not even buried in America.

In 1961, after a lifetime of struggle, W.E.B. Du Bois renounced his American citizenship, joined the Communist party, and emigrated to Ghana, the first ex-colonial black African nation. Du Bois died there in 1963 at the age of ninety-five. His influence on America's civil-rights movement has been felt by every black leader in this country.

Du Bois was born in Great Barrington, Massachusetts, in 1868 and was the most influential black American for more than half a century. His book *The Souls of Black Folk*, published in 1903, accurately predicted that the most pressing issue facing America in the twentieth century would be race relations. His book went further than just predicting the civil-rights movement; it outlined a plan of action for black Americans — a plan that is as valid today as the day it was written.

Du Bois promoted political action as a means of changing racist practices in America. He demanded the right to vote, called for an end to segregation, advocated more funding for the education of black Americans, and called for the adoption of laws guaranteeing civil rights.

". . . despite compromise, war, and struggle, the Negro is not free," Du Bois said.

He believed that the only way black Americans could attain equality was through agitation and education. The battle, he said, would be fought with "the weapons of Truth, with the sword of the intrepid, uncompromising Spirit."

The policy advocated in *The Souls of Black Folk*, and in his other writings, was in direct conflict with the teachings of Booker T. Washington (1856–1915), the foremost black leader of the period. It was Du Bois's opinion that Washington was a compromiser. His policies of accommodation denied black Americans their fundamental rights, Du Bois maintained.

In his essay "Of Mr. Booker T. Washington and Others," which appeared in the controversial *Souls of Black Folk*, Du Bois attacked Washington as a timid leader more concerned with his own prestige than with the plight of his people. This attack shook the foundation of the civil-rights movement in America by bringing to the forefront the issue of how black Americans should achieve freedom and equality.

"Mr. Washington represents in the Negro thought, the old attitude of adjustment and submission," Du Bois wrote.

Du Bois demanded far more than accommodation and gradual results. He saw self-respect among black Americans as the foundation for change and could not see in Washington's policies any means of achieving that.

"In the history of nearly all other races and peoples the doctrine preached at such crises has been that manly self-respect is worth more than lands and houses, and that a people who voluntarily surrender such respect, or cease striving for it, are not worth civilizing," Du Bois wrote.

The Souls of Black Folk was not merely an attack on the policies of Booker T. Washington. It was a wake-up call for black Americans, demanding that blacks take their destiny into their own hands through political action and education. Without political action and education, Du Bois believed that black Americans would give up their rightful place in America.

He saw the future of black America belonging to educated leaders. He believed that the best black scholars, whom he referred to as the "Talented Tenth" (of the black population), should be educated in the best colleges and universities to provide leadership for the black masses.

"The problem of education, then, among Negroes must first of all deal with the Talented Tenth; it is the problem of developing the Best of this race, that they may guide the masses away from the contamination and death of the Worst; in their own and other races," he wrote.

The greatest need Du Bois saw was for colleges to train black teachers. Their goal would be to "furnish the Black world with adequate standards of human culture and lofty ideals of life." It was largely because of Du Bois's advocacy for more education that black colleges like Howard, Spelman, and Lincoln University expanded.

There were fourteen chapters to *The Souls of Black Folk*, each an independent essay displaying a varied range of genres. Interwoven throughout the text were bits of history, poetry, music, economic analysis, social commentary, religion, and fables, all held together with Du Bois's unequivocal advocacy for political action. Its format was far more contemporary than any book of its time.

When it was published, *The Souls of Black Folk* was considered the most dangerous book in America and was banned in many southern states. Still, it has maintained its relevancy and popularity, having gone through more than thirty editions since its initial publication. Many black-history scholars hail it as the greatest book on the plight of black America, rivaled only by *Uncle Tom's Cabin*.

Du Bois aimed the book specifically at black Americans as an impassioned plea for unconditional equality.

"Work, culture, liberty — all these we need, not singly but together, not successively, but together, each growing and aiding each. . . ." he wrote.

Du Bois did not want to "Africanize America," but rather, "to make it possible for a man to be both a Negro and an American, without being cursed and spit upon by his fellows, without having the doors of Opportunity closed roughly in his face."

He attended Fisk University and later went to Harvard University, where he received his Ph.D. in 1895. He studied in Berlin and later served as professor of sociology at Atlanta University from 1897 to 1910.

Besides his writings, Du Bois was instrumental in the

founding of the Niagara Movement, formed in 1905 at Niagara Falls, New York. The movement was made up of prominent black leaders whose goal was to establish a force for political and economic action. In 1909, the Niagara Movement merged with a white liberal New York group to form the biracial National Association for the Advancement of Colored People (NAACP). From 1910 until 1934, Du Bois served as the editor for the NAACP's magazine, *The Crisis*, where he was an outspoken advocate for political action.

Du Bois joined an international peace movement in the early 1950s and became a Socialist. He was indicted by the U.S. Department of Justice in 1951 for his so-called subversive work on behalf of the International Peace Information Center. Although he was acquitted of the charges against him, he spent the latter half of the decade in the Soviet Union and China. In 1958, Du Bois was awarded the Lenin Peace Prize, and in 1961 he officially joined the American Communist party.

"I believe in communism. I mean by communism a planned way of life in the production of wealth and work designed for building a state whose object is the highest welfare of its people and not merely the profit of a part," he wrote.

In 1961, he renounced his American citizenship and moved to Ghana, where he is buried.

His contribution to the civil-rights movement in America has had a long and far-reaching impact, influencing every major civil-rights leader from Malcolm X to Martin Luther King, Jr.

35 Lincoln Steffens (1866–1936)
The Shame of the Cities, 1904

"The world is for workers, not for tourists."

THE TIMES: The American Academy of Arts and Letters was founded. *The Sea Wolf* by Jack London was published. O. Henry published his first collection of short stories, *Cabbages and Kings*. Cy Young of the American League Boston Americans pitched the first perfect baseball game. The first Olympic Games were held in America in St. Louis, Missouri. The first auto race was held in Long Island, New York. Teddy Roosevelt was reelected president.

Lincoln Steffens's book *The Shame of the Cities*, published in 1904, was the first major exposé on municipal corruption and won Steffens the honor of being known as the first and foremost "muckraker"—a term coined by President Theodore Roosevelt (1858–1919).

Unlike other so-called muckrakers of the period, Steffens claimed he was was not trying to present a sensationalist exposé. He was more concerned with understanding the nature of the cities, the politicians who ran them, and the people who lived in them. His work was not a condemnation of the inner workings of city government but a sociological study.

"What I want is to gain a deeper insight into the heart of my day," Steffens said.

Although he received a Ph.D. in philosophy from the University of California in 1884, and studied philosophy in Europe for several years, he was not concerned with the philosophical bent of the world.

"I seek the striving, struggling, battling practical world which far outranks the philosophical heavens," he said.

According to Steffens, ". . . the world is for workers, not for tourists."

The Shame of the Cities was a collection of articles that Steffens published while he was with *McClure's Magazine*. The first of these articles was published in 1902. Called "Tweed Days in St. Louis," it was written in collaboration with St. Louis reporter Claude Wetmore. The article was about a crusading St. Louis attorney, Joseph Folk, who was trying to clean up a den of corrupt elected officials in that city.

Steffens was an editor at *McClure's* at the time. When Wetmore filed his story, Steffens felt it wasn't hard-hitting enough and revised it. The revisions were extensive enough to warrant a by-line by Steffens, and so began Lincoln Steffens's career as the country's first and leading "muckraker."

Theodore Roosevelt created the term "muckraker" in 1906. He meant it as a condemnation of journalists who specialized in sensationalist exposés of business and government.

But true "muckrakers" like Steffens had loftier goals. They were not merely concerned with bringing out into the open the corrupt practices of businesses and elected officials; they wanted to find practical solutions to the problems they uncovered.

"My writing is not important . . . finding out things is very important," Steffens said.

Steffens followed up his first article with one called "The Shamelessness of St. Louis." It covered the life and times of Edward Butler, a St. Louis ward boss who ruled the city and had made a fortune through bribes. Butler was ultimately tried and convicted to three years in the state prison because of Steffens's article.

This was followed by "The Shame of Minneapolis," in which Steffens chronicled a grand-jury investigation into the corrupt administration of Mayor Albert Alonzo Ames. Despite bribery and extortion charges against Ames, many people in Minneapolis came to the defense of the corrupt mayor and opposed the work of the reform-minded grand jury.

"No reform has failed to bring out this phenomenon of virtuous cowardice, the baseness of the decent citizen," Steffens said.

Steffens's articles covered thirteen cities in thirteen states. While the series was running, the circulation of *McClure's* soared to more than five hundred thousand. When *The Shame of the Cities* was published in 1904, it caused an immediate sensation. Ultimately, it became the most influential reform publication of its day. Steffens did not care about incarcerating corrupt public officials. He asked, instead, for understanding and became friends with many of the politicians he exposed in his book.

Based on his extensive research on the workings of American cities, Steffens concluded that corruption was at every level of government, but that the fault did not lie with those accepting bribes, but rather with the American people for not becoming actively involved in the affairs of their own governments.

"The misgovernment of the American people is misgovernment by the American people," Steffens said.

"[W]e all think that we shall devise some day a legal machine that will turn out good government automatically," he explained.

Although *The Shame of the Cities* led to major reforms in city and state governments across the country, Steffens became more and more skeptical of reforms that simply punished corrupt leaders. The American people, he felt, actively avoided involving themselves in the process of self-government, and because of that, he viewed reform movements as short-term solutions.

Born in San Francisco in April 1866, Lincoln Steffens was the youngest child and only boy in the family of five children. He failed his final year in grammar school and was sent to a military academy, where his grades were so poor, he was refused admission into college. After a year of tutoring, he was finally accepted at the University of California in 1885. Although he graduated in 1889, Steffens had little use for formal education.

"Damn these universities, all of them. They have made my life one of unlearning literally. . . ." he said.

Steffens told his life story in his book *Autobiography*, published in 1931. He once said he wanted to call the book "A Life of Unlearning." *Autobiography* is still considered a monumental work of memoir writing.

After his graduation from the University of California, Steffens went to Germany to study philosophy. In 1892, he landed a position as a reporter for the New York *Evening Post*. At the *Post*, he was befriended by Jacob Riis (1849–1914), the author of the impassioned chronicle of America's poor *How the Other Half Lives* (1890). Steffens wrote many other reform-minded exposés, but none with the impact of *The Shame of the Cities*.

He suffered a heart attack in 1933 and remained confined to bed for the next three years. He died in August 1936 at the age of seventy.

The *San Francisco Chronicle* wrote of Steffens, "No other journalist of our time has used his power with more consistent devotion to the principles of human justice."

Ida Tarbell (1857–1944)
36 *The History of the Standard Oil Company*, 1904

"To my chagrin I found myself included in a new school, that of the muckrakers."

THE TIMES: *The Virginian*, written by Owen Wister, was published and became one of the most popular western novels of all time. More than three hundred thousand copies of the book were sold within the first year. Helen Keller published her autobiography, *The Story of My Life*. The Davis Cup international tennis championship was held for the first time in Boston, Massachusetts. *The Clansman*, by Thomas Dixon, was published. It was the basis for D. W. Griffith's controversial movie *The Birth of a Nation*.

Ida Tarbell never intended to force the breakup of one of America's biggest corporations with her two-volume book *The History of the Standard Oil Company*, but that's exactly what happened!

Published in 1904, *The History of the Standard Oil Company* took five years for Tarbell to write. It appeared first as a series of nineteen articles in *McClure's Magazine* from 1901 to 1904. Tarbell began the series of articles as a historic account of

John D. Rockefeller's oil interests and an examination of the oil trust as an economic force in American society. Tarbell set out to write a factual narrative of America's largest industry and was adamant about presenting an accurate and fair picture, through precise documentation. Tarbell wanted the story to be "received as a legitimate historical study."

The readership of *McClure's* and her editors and fellow writers wanted more than a "historical study."

"I soon found that most of them wanted attacks. They had little interest in balanced findings," she said.

Tarbell began her work with an open mind, not even sure that Rockefeller had done anything dishonest in his dealings with Standard Oil. There was already a body of information available showing that trusts — giant corporations like Standard Oil — had used unsavory and often illegal tactics, including bribery and threats, to drive competitors out of the business and guarantee a monopoly. Standard Oil was the biggest trust in America at the time, and John D. Rockefeller the most powerful and wealthy man in the country.

Tarbell had experienced the tactics of Standard Oil in her own life. Her father, Franklin Tarbell, a once-prosperous independent oilman, and her brother had been financially ruined by Standard Oil. Still, Tarbell maintained she was not out for vengeance — only truth. The truth that Tarbell uncovered changed the American business world forever.

Although he was retired, Rockefeller continued to run the operations of Standard Oil from his home. At the time the articles appeared, Rockefeller employed more people in his business than the sum total of the U.S. Army. Rockefeller, who tried first to ignore Tarbell's series of articles, soon found himself and his company reviled by the public and hounded by increased demands by the government to set controls on the industry. He disdainfully called her "Miss Tarbarrel."

Her father had warned her that Rockefeller would stop at nothing. When she told her father about the series of articles she planned, Franklin Tarbell warned her, "Don't do it. He will ruin the magazine."

And Rockefeller tried. One of his banks threatened the financial status of the magazine. Tarbell was confronted directly by one of the bank's vice presidents, who implied that financial support for the magazine might vanish unless her articles ceased.

"Of course, that makes no difference to me," Tarbell told the shocked vice president.

But it was not just threats that stood in the way of Tarbell doing her work. She began her research for the book by studying the stacks of government records on Standard Oil. Congressional committees had investigated Rockefeller's holdings in 1872, 1876, 1879, and 1891 — but many of the important documents were missing. People refused to be interviewed. A wall of silence went up around Standard Oil and the people who had dealings with it.

Her research was slow and painstaking. One of the key documents in Tarbell's investigation was called *The Rise and Fall of the South Improvement Company*, written in 1873. It spelled out in minute detail the dealings of the company, which had combined with the railroads to regulate shipping prices in its favor and provide illegal information about competitors' oil shipments. By doing so, the South Improvement Company was able to drive independent oil refiners out of business — independents like Ida Tarbell's father.

The Standard Oil Company had risen out of the ashes of the disbanded South Improvement Company, and nothing was more damning for John D. Rockefeller than to be associated with the South Improvement Company's illegal schemes. All the copies of *The Rise and Fall of the South Improvement Company* were gone. Standard Oil had bought up and destroyed all of them, or so its executives thought.

"Under the combined threat and persuasion of the Standard, armed with the South Improvement Company scheme, almost the entire independent oil interest of Cleveland collapsed ... of the 26 refiners, at least 21 sold out," Tarbell wrote. Throughout its underhanded dealings, Standard Oil gained a monopoly on the oil-refining industry in America.

Although Standard Oil did its best to thwart Tarbell's research, she found one remaining copy of the South Improvement Company report tucked away in the New York Public Library. In that precious document, she was able to identify John D. Rockefeller as the driving force behind the South Improvement Company's illegal tactics. Further evidence showed that Rockefeller bought the company in 1871 and had all the parties involved sign a pledge of secrecy. Tarbell discovered secret agreements that Rockefeller had with the railroads aimed at destroying all competition and leading to Standard Oil's monopoly on the industry.

Month after month in *McClure's Magazine*, Tarbell's articles laid bare the illegal, corrupt, and greedy schemes of one of America's biggest corporations. The series of articles were a sensation in America and in Europe. *McClure's* was flooded with mail praising the work of this brave reporter. Tarbell became known as "the Queen of the Muckrakers," and "the Joan of Arc of the Oil Industry" — titles that Tarbell disavowed. She did not think of herself as a reform-minded crusader. She wanted only to present the truth. Despite herself, she became an international celebrity.

The History of the Standard Oil Company was published in 1904 and appeared in two volumes, with over twenty-one hundred pages of documentation. It became an immediate best-seller — "the most remarkable book of its kind ever written in this country," one reviewer said.

But Tarbell's book did more than become a best-seller. It brought about the dissolution of Standard Oil and led to legislation to police American businesses so that such illegal practices could never again lead to monopolies such as Standard Oil had.

In 1906, the government began proceedings against Standard Oil. In 1911, following a series of appeals by the company, the Standard Oil Company was dissolved and its monopoly on America's oil industry broken forever. Because of Tarbell's book, the government enacted the Hepburn Act in 1906 to oversee railroads and oil companies. In 1910 came the Mann-Elkins Act, which gave the Interstate Commerce Commission control over oil rates. In 1914, the Federal Trade Commission Act was created to oversee business practices, and the Clayton Antitrust Act — which forever prohibited unfair competition leading to monopolies like Standard Oil's — was passed.

The History of the Standard Oil Company remains as a masterpiece of investigative journalism.

Tarbell, who was born November 1857 in Erie County, Pennsylvania, spent the rest of her life writing and lecturing. None of her later work had as much success as *The History of the Standard Oil Company*.

After attending Allegheny College, she worked as a writer for and then managing editor of the *Chautauquan* magazine. She spent from 1891 to 1894 studying at the Sorbonne in Paris. After her work at *McClure's*, she became the associate editor of *The American Magazine* from 1906 to 1915.

She died in Bridgeport, Connecticut, at eighty-seven and is buried in her hometown of Titusville, Pennsylvania.

37 Upton Sinclair (1878–1968)
The Jungle, 1906

> *"They use everything about the hog except the squeal."*

THE TIMES: May Sutton was the first American woman to win the Wimbledon singles title in tennis. The San Francisco Earthquake destroyed over two hundred thousand buildings, causing an estimated $350 million in damage. President Teddy Roosevelt won the Nobel Peace Prize. The Ziegfeld Follies opened in New York. The Follies ran for twenty-four years.

Upton Sinclair's book took dead aim at the heart of America's social consciousness, but missed. Instead, it made a direct hit on America's collective stomach.

The Jungle, published in 1906, tells the story of the ruthless exploitation of a family of Lithuanian immigrants working in the stockyard district of Chicago. Sinclair intended the book as an indictment against working-class conditions, and a call to action for the working class. What he got instead was national legislation in the form of both the Pure Food and Drug Act and the Beef Inspection Act, both passed within six months of the publication of the book.

Ironically, little more than twelve pages out of the entire three-hundred-plus pages of *The Jungle* had anything to do with the unsavory accounts of meat production—but those mere twelve pages were enough to turn the stomachs of most Americans, including President Theodore Roosevelt.

Among the gruesome accounts Sinclair offered up to the reading public was the sale of tubercular steers in the marketplace; poisoned rats ground up and passed off as ground beef; lard made up of hogs afflicted with cholera; and accounts of workers falling into boiling kettles, their remains being sold as top-quality lard.

"They don't waste anything here," Sinclair wrote. "They use everything about the hog except the squeal."

The country was sickened and angered by the accounts and demanded reform of the meat-packing industry.

Author Jack London (1876–1916) hailed Sinclair's book as a benchmark for Socialism in America. "What *Uncle Tom's Cabin* did for the black slaves, *The Jungle* has a large chance to do for the white slaves. . . ." London proclaimed.

Upton Sinclair published five novels from 1901 to 1904, none of which was commercially successful. He was twenty-seven years old when he was given a small advance by the Socialist weekly *An Appeal to Reason* to investigate the conditions of workers in the Chicago stockyards. Sinclair spent seven weeks in the stockyards living among the workers, gathering material, before returning to New Jersey to write *The Jungle*.

The writing of the book took a personal toll on Sinclair. He was nearly penniless and depressed over his faltering literary career. His baby almost died of pneumonia, and his wife attempted suicide. He and his family were living in a small, cold house. Things couldn't have been bleaker. Still, Sinclair continued his investigation into the Chicago stockyards.

"I sat at night in the homes of the workers, foreign born

and native, and they told me their stories. . . . I would wander about the yards, and their friends would risk their jobs to show me what I wanted to see," Sinclair said.

He completed the book in less than a year. It was first serialized in *An Appeal to Reason*, but word of this powerful story spread quickly. The editors at the magazine couldn't keep up with the demand for copies.

"I wrote with tears and anguish, pouring into the pages all that pain which life had meant to me," Sinclair said about the book.

Despite its appeal, *The Jungle* was rejected by the first five publishers that Sinclair offered it to. All of them felt the book was too dangerous. The meat-packing industry was a powerful lobby in America. It wasn't about to back away from the hard-hitting charges brought against it by Sinclair.

Unable to get any of the top publishing houses to issue the book, Sinclair asked readers of *An Appeal to Reason* to order and pay for copies of the book in advance. He received over twelve thousand orders for the book and prepared it for publication himself. Finally, sensing a best-seller in the making, Doubleday, Page and Company offered to publish the book if Sinclair could prove the authenticity of his charges against the meat-packing industry. A former meat inspector at the stockyards who had been fired for stopping the sale of diseased meat verified Sinclair's charges and told the editors at Doubleday, Page that there were far worse things going on in the stockyards.

The book was published in January 1906, and the story sent shock waves through the meat-packing industry. It became an instant best-seller in both America and England and was translated into more than a dozen languages. It sold more than 150,000 copies.

President Theodore Roosevelt was so enraged by the book,

he ordered a major investigation into the meat-packing industry. The industry denied the charges in *The Jungle* and fought back. First it attempted to discredit Sinclair, claiming the author was simply seeking notoriety at its expense. The industry enlisted magazines and newspapers sympathetic to its position to refute Sinclair's claims. *The Saturday Evening Post* attacked Sinclair, as did the *Chicago Tribune* and several Boston-based newspapers. The meat-packing industry spent enormous sums of money advertising, in an attempt to present its side of the story. Industry lobbyists worked overtime trying to find friendly supporters in Congress.

As the industry attacked, President Roosevelt counterattacked. He sent a blue-ribbon commission to Chicago to look into the conditions of the industry. They returned with a scathing report condemning the meat-packing practices. The report further fueled the public's outcry for reform. Finally, the public spoke with its pocketbooks. Meat consumption nearly came to a halt. When confronted with this bleak economic outlook, the meat-packing industry ended its holdout, and Congress passed both laws to oversee the meat-packing industry.

A year after the Pure Food and Drug Act and the Beef Inspection Act were passed, a study of the meat-packing industry found many of the unsanitary practices were still being used. Although Sinclair's book had forced the passage of the legislation, enforcement of the laws was a long way off.

More than thirty years later, studies of the industry still showed only minor progress. Although many states had laws governing the inspection of meat, many of the laws were inadequate, and enforcement was practically nonexistent. In 1967, Congress enacted the Wholesale Meat Act, which forced all states to meet federal guidelines. President Lyndon Johnson invited Upton Sinclair to Washington to take part in the signing of the act.

Sinclair made close to thirty thousand dollars from *The Jungle*, and he used all the money to build his own utopian community residence at Helicon Hall in New Jersey, where writers and artists could come and stay. John Dewey, William James, and Sinclair Lewis were all guests there. The hall burned down, and Sinclair lost everything with it.

Sinclair was born in Baltimore in 1878, an only child. He went through eight grades of public school in two years. He went to the College of the City of New York (1892–97) and then went to graduate school at Columbia, where he earned a meager living selling jokes and writing for the dime novels of the day. Sinclair would reportedly write an astounding eight thousand words a night while in graduate school, cranking out approximately two good-sized dime novels a month. He was offered an appointment to the Naval Academy, but refused and instead studied to become a lawyer. His hack writing led to a job writing for a popular magazine, *Starry Flag Library*.

In 1890, he wrote and self-published his first novel, *Springtime and Harvest*, which was a financial failure. Sinclair met George Herron, a socialist editor who enlisted him in the socialist movement. In 1904, Sinclair wrote *Manassas*, called by Jack London "the best Civil War book I've read."

Sinclair remained an active socialist all his life. Besides his writing, he ran for Congress in 1906 in New Jersey, founded the American Civil Liberties Union in California, and later ran for Congress in that state, for the Senate in 1922, and for governor in 1926 and 1930. In 1934, running on a platform designed to end poverty in California, he received the Democratic nomination and ran for governor. He never won a single election.

During his career, Sinclair published many of his books at his own expense and helped found the Vanguard Press, which was dedicated to publishing books at prices working men and women could afford. In 1942, he won the Pulitzer Prize for *Dragon's Teeth*.

Throughout his life, Upton Sinclair remained true to his socialist ideals. According to Sinclair, he wrote "exclusively in the cause of human welfare."

He was one of America's most prolific writers, with ninety books to his credit, and he remains the most widely read American author in Europe. More than 2 million copies of his books have been sold in Germany and 3 million in Russia.

"When I wrote about what really interested me, I never stopped for day or night for weeks at a time," Sinclair said.

His writing stopped in 1968, when he died at the age of ninety.

38

Samuel Hopkins Adams
(1871–1958)
The Great American Fraud, 1906

"I could ask nothing better than the life of a professional writer."

THE TIMES: Zane Grey published his first western novel. In his lifetime, Grey wrote sixty books that sold more than 13 million copies. New Orleans ragtime piano player "Jelly Roll" Morton was a hit across the country. The first radio broadcast was made by Reginald Fessenden in Massachusetts. Devil's Tower in Wyoming was named as the first national monument. Henry Adams self-published *The Education of Henry Adams*. Adams received a Nobel Prize for his work in 1919.

One good dose of Samuel Hopkins Adams's book *The Great American Fraud* helped cure the patent-medicine industry of its ailments. Adams's book inspired the passage in 1906 of the Pure Food and Drug Act, which protected the American people from medical quackery and fraudulent drug remedies.

Adams worked as a reporter for *McClure's Magazine*, where he wrote several articles on the social impact of several diseases and their treatments. He is credited with being the first writer to popularize medical writing.

"Having become interested in medical science, I made public health my specialty," Adams said.

He followed his work at *McClure's* with a series of articles exposing the abuses in the patent-medicine industry and on fraudulent medical practices. The articles were published in *Collier's* weekly magazine in 1905. The series of articles in *Collier's*, later published in 1906 in book form as *The Great American Fraud*, was credited with furthering the passage of the first Pure Food and Drug Act.

Among the abuses Adams highlighted was the sale of untested drugs to the public, including the sale of such poisons as arsenic. Adams also argued for accurate labeling on medicines, since some supposed "cure-alls" were simply pure alcohol and had no true medicinal purpose.

"The public has the right to know," Adams said.

He also exposed the use of narcotics, sold as family remedies, and the abuses of unlicensed medical practitioners, who often posed as physicians. Adams cited incidents where patients, among them children, had died as the result of quack patent medicines.

Congress had been slow to act, despite the widespread and documented threat to the American public at the hands of unscrupulous medical quacks and through the use of untested medicines.

In 1906, Adams's series of articles was issued in book form by the American Medical Association (AMA), under the title of *The Great American Fraud*. Copies of the book were distributed to leading members of Congress. The AMA, which had been tainted by the abuses and by those posing as doctors, demanded that Congress regulate the patent-medicine industry.

In June 1906, the Pure Food and Drug Act was passed by

Congress. Adams's book *The Great American Fraud* was cited on the floor of the U.S. House of Representatives as being one of the most influential arguments for regulating the drug industry. The Pure Food and Drug Act prohibited the sale of adulterated foods and drugs and required labeling on drugs, listing the contents.

Ironically, on the same day, Congress passed the Meat Inspection Act, which required sanitary conditions and federal inspection of all meat-packing plants engaged in interstate commerce. Upton Sinclair (1878–1968), the author of *The Jungle*, an exposé on the Chicago meat-packing industry, and a friend of Adams, was credited with bringing about the passage of the bill.

In 1913, the AMA made Adams an associate member; he was one of the few nonmedical people to be awarded this distinction.

Adams went on to write nearly fifty books in his long career, many of them best-sellers. "Certainly writing is work. Hard work. But so is any craft. I rewrite everything at least three times," Adams said.

Seventeen of his books were adapted for the movies. Among them, his short story "Night Bus" appeared on the silver screen as *It Happened One Night*, starring Clark Gable and Claudette Colbert, and won an Oscar for Best Picture in 1934.

"Some fifteen or sixteen of my stories have been done into movies; some with a result so painful that I have been unable to sit through the presentation; one, at least, 'It Happened One Night,' improved in the adaptation, and was directed and acted with such artistry and verve that I should like to see it again," Adams said.

Adams was also the author of the novel *Flaming Youth*,

published in 1923. The novel depicted the turmoil of the Jazz Age of the 1920s. Adams wrote the book under the pseudonym "Warner Fabian."

"I knew it was a book that could make a helluva lot of money, but I didn't want my own name on it," Adams said.

His writing career spanned seventy years. He was born in Dunkirk, New York, in 1871 and began writing poetry at sixteen years old while he was a student at Hamilton College in New York. He graduated from Hamilton in 1891. He worked as a reporter for the *New York Sun* for eight years before joining *McClure's Magazine*.

"I could ask nothing better than the life of a professional writer. It permits freedom of thought, action and mode of existence, and this in an era when individual choice threatened as it is throughout an imperiled world, has never been so precious," Adams said.

He died in 1958 in Beaufort, South Carolina, at the age of eighty-seven.

39 Margaret Sanger (1883–1966)
Family Limitation, 1914

> *"To instruct women in the things they need to know."*

THE TIMES: America entered the war. The first American troops landed in France. Poet Carl Sandburg published his first book of verse, *Chicago Poems*. The Eighteenth Amendment to the Constitution was enacted, prohibiting the manufacturing, sale, and transportation of liquor. The first Pulitzer prizes were awarded. *My Ántonia* by Willa Cather was published. The play *Lightnin'* opened on Broadway. It ran for more than twelve hundred performances, one of the longest runs in stage history. Kaiser Wilhelm II of Germany abdicated, bringing an end to World War I.

In 1914, Margaret Sanger wrote an article on birth control for a small Socialist newspaper. The title of that article was "What Every Girl Should Know." Copies of the newspaper were confiscated by the U.S. Postal Service and returned to Sanger with the word NOTHING scrawled across the title of her article. This was the beginning of a lifelong battle by Sanger to educate women about safe birth-control methods.

Sanger coined the term "birth control" in the United States, and she was a tireless crusader for women's rights to control their own reproductive destiny. Through her writings and efforts, laws prohibiting the distribution of information on contraception were repealed and safe birth-control clinics were established throughout the world.

"The problem of birth control has arisen directly from the effort of the feminine spirit to free itself from bondage," Sanger said.

In 1914, she published her own magazine, *The Woman Rebel*, which advocated the use of birth control and the right to distribute information about it. "No Gods, No Masters" was the magazine's slogan. According to Sanger, she published the magazine to "stimulate working women to think for themselves, and to build up a conscious fighting character."

Copies of *The Woman Rebel* were confiscated by the U.S. Postal Service. The Comstock Law of 1873 made it a crime to send obscene material through the mails, and information about contraception was deemed obscene by the U.S. government, the Roman Catholic Church, and by most major businesses in the country.

In 1914, Sanger published a birth-control pamphlet, *Family Limitation*, which was also confiscated by the U.S. Postal Service.

Sanger had approached two dozen publishers trying to get the *Family Limitation* pamphlet printed, but she was turned down by all of them. Publishers were afraid they would be indicted under the Comstock Law provisions. Finally, the printer who had produced her first magazine agreed. As soon as the pamphlet was released, Sanger was arrested and charged with mailing illegal materials.

Sanger's lawyer suggested that she plead guilty to the

charges in exchange for a lesser sentence, but Sanger refused, saying she had deliberately broken the law.

"The law was wrong, not I," she said.

If convicted of the charges against her, Sanger could have faced up to forty-five years in prison. She asked the courts to grant her a continuance to prepare her defense, and when they refused her request, Sanger fled to Canada. Her supporters in Canada provided help by hiding her and by publishing and smuggling into the United States copies of the *Family Limitation* pamphlet.

Over the next year, she traveled freely through England, France, Spain, and other parts of Europe, studying the various birth-control techniques of these countries. In Holland, she studied the small but growing planned-parenthood clinics. She learned that both infant and maternal mortalities had been reduced in that country through the use of the clinics. It was then that she decided to return to the United States and begin her crusade again, this time focusing on the establishment of clinics as a way of providing safe birth-control services and education.

She returned to America in 1915. During her self-imposed exile, interest in her cause had grown to near epic proportions. A letter, signed by many of the country's leading reformers and intellectuals, was sent to President Wilson, protesting the charges against Sanger. Soon, protests throughout the country erupted, calling for the charges against Sanger to be dropped. The government dropped the charges against Sanger, and her case never came to trial.

Her victory was bittersweet. Although the government had dropped the charges, it had not changed the Comstock Law, prohibiting the distribution of birth-control information. Sanger decided upon another, more radical approach.

In 1916, with the help of her sister, who was like Sanger herself a trained nurse, she opened this country's first birth-control clinic in the poorest section of Brooklyn, New York. It was Sanger's intent to establish clinics throughout the country, staffed by trained medical professionals who would "instruct women in the things they need to know."

More than two hundred women were at the front doors of Sanger's clinic on the day it opened. Nine days later, the clinic was closed by New York authorities. Sanger was arrested and charged with violating the New York Penal Code, which prohibited the distribution of birth-control information, and for maintaining a public nuisance.

In court, Sanger refused the judges' demand that she promise to obey the law. Sanger explained to the judge that she could not respect a law that prohibited women from taking control of their own lives. Sanger was found guilty and sentenced to thirty days in prison. While incarcerated at the Long Island prison, Sanger busied herself by teaching other prisoners how to read and write.

Her subsequent appeal resulted in a decision handed down by the United States Court of Appeals in 1918 that allowed physicians to give birth-control information to women for the purpose of the cure and prevention of disease. This was a major breakthrough for Sanger and the birth-control movement in America. Women in America could now receive information on birth-control methods.

After her release from prison, Sanger traveled the country to publicize the importance of birth control. In the early 1920s, she made several unsuccessful attempts at passing legislation that would promote birth-control education. Her bills failed in New York, New Jersey, and Connecticut, but because of her efforts, the birth-control movement in America began to grow.

In 1923, she opened her second birth-control clinic in New York City. Six years after it opened, the police raided the clinic and seized all the medical records. This proved to be a fatal mistake by the New York authorities. The New York Medical Society came to Sanger's defense, claiming the confiscation of the records constituted a violation of medical ethics. The case against Sanger was dropped.

In 1939, Sanger helped form the Birth Control Federation of America, which in 1942 became the Planned Parenthood Federation of America. Sanger was installed as Planned Parenthood's first president and went on to help establish birth-control organizations in both India and Japan.

Margaret Sanger was born in Corning, New York, in 1883. She attended Claverack College, but left school and returned home to care for her mother, who later died of tuberculosis. After her mother's death, she set her sights on a nursing career and began study at the White Plains Hospital in New York. She completed her training at the Manhattan Eye and Ear Hospital.

Following her graduation, she married William Sanger, an artist, who introduced her to the Socialist party. Sanger began writing articles on health care for several Socialist publications. She worked as a nurse in the poverty-stricken Lower East Side, where she saw firsthand the misery faced by women who had no access to safe birth-control methods.

It was at this point in her life that she decided to quit nursing and devote her life to the birth-control movement in America. She died in September 1966 at the age of eighty-two.

40 John Steinbeck (1902–68)
The Grapes of Wrath, 1939

"The ancient commission of the writer has not changed."

THE TIMES: Walt Disney's film classic *Snow White and the Seven Dwarfs* was released. *Our Town* by Thornton Wilder was published. Orson Welles broadcast his "War of the Worlds" radio program, causing panic throughout the country. Pearl Buck became the first American woman to win the Nobel Prize for Literature for her book *The Good Earth*. Germany invaded Poland. England and France declared war on Germany. The movie *Gone With the Wind* was released.

Despite winning a Pulitzer Prize for his masterful depiction of the plight of landless farm laborers in *The Grapes of Wrath*, published in 1939, and despite becoming only the sixth American writer to win the Nobel Prize for Literature, John Steinbeck has had only a lukewarm reputation among literary critics in America.

With the announcement that Steinbeck would be the 1962 recipient of the Nobel Prize came a flurry of negative literary criticism. *Newsweek* magazine called *The Grapes of Wrath* a limited work of fiction, saying it was "scarcely able to survive its time and place." In another national publication, it was observed that "three of the six Nobel awards to Americans have gone to writers who, far from being nationally esteemed among the finest of their time, are not even considered first-rate."

Despite the attacks against Steinbeck and his collected works, *The Grapes of Wrath* still ranks as one of the best American novels. When asked what the major function of an author was, Steinbeck said, "Criticism, I should think."

Although he wrote a number of best-selling novels during his lifetime, it was *The Grapes of Wrath* that was largely responsible for his winning the Nobel Prize. It is a story about the exploitation of an indigent family of farm workers, the Joads, who leave their home in Oklahoma and travel to California in the hopes of beginning their lives over. The story of the Joad family is interspersed with descriptive background information about the country during the Depression era of the 1930s.

The Dust Bowl drought and the failing economy force the Joads to leave Oklahoma and head west to California, where they expect to earn a living as farm workers. During the late 1930s, thousands of migrants from the Midwest headed for California in search of a better life. Steinbeck witnessed first-hand the brutal treatment of these poor families at the hands of the authorities and unscrupulous farm owners and dedicated himself to writing a book that would expose their plight. The result was *The Grapes of Wrath*.

"I want to put a tag of shame on the greedy bastards who are responsible for this, but I can best do it through newspapers," Steinbeck said.

The book became the most controversial and influential novel of the Depression era. It has been favorably compared to Upton Sinclair's *The Jungle* and Harriet Beecher Stowe's

Uncle Tom's Cabin for its ability to chronicle the social conditions of the times. It was not viewed as a novel, but as a document of fact. Critics examined the book not as a work of fiction but as a nonfiction account of the migrant farm workers' plight.

The book was denounced on the floor of the United States Senate as anti-American and was banned from many libraries across the country for being obscene. As late as the 1990s, *The Grapes of Wrath* remained one of the most censored books in the country. It was attacked for its brutal language and factual inaccuracies. Some critics called it communistic propaganda. "A black, infernal creation of a twisted, distorted mind," wrote one reviewer. California farm owners were outraged, saying that Steinbeck had slandered them. And even religious leaders joined in the attack, claiming Steinbeck had presented a distorted view of America and its people.

Despite the controversy surrounding the book, it was an enormous literary and financial success and quickly became a best-seller. No book better captured the tenor of the Depression or the frustrations Americans felt.

Steinbeck prepared for writing the book by touring the itinerant laborers' camps in California. He picked produce in the fields alongside field workers and traveled across the country with Oklahoma farm workers who were heading to California to find work. His firsthand experiences and observations formed the basis for the book.

"Men stood by their fences and looked at the ruined corn, drying fast now, only a little green showing through the film of dust. The men were silent and they did not move often. And the women came out of the houses to stand beside their men — to feel whether this time the men would break. The women studied the men's faces secretly, for the corn could go, so long as something else remained," Steinbeck wrote.

In other sections, he depicted the wealthy men and women in America as oblivious to the plight of the farmers and the poor.

He described them as "Languid, heat-raddled ladies, small nucleuses about whom revolve a thousand accouterments: creams, ointments to grease themselves, coloring matter in phials — black, pink, red, white, green, silver — to change the color of hair, eyes, lips, nails, brows, lashes, lids. Oils, seeds and pills to make the bowels move."

Their husbands didn't fare much better.

"Beside them, little pot-bellied men in light suits and panama hats; clean, pink men with puzzled, worried eyes, with restless eyes. Worried because formulas do not work out; hungry for security and yet sensing its disappearance from the earth," he wrote.

Steinbeck angered politicians by advocating a government that arises out of the immediate needs of the people and stays in a constant state of revolution to meet the changing needs of the people it is supposed to serve.

Despite the stark realism of the book and its bleak ending, Steinbeck had faith that society could overcome the most devastating economic obstacles and natural disasters.

"I hold that a writer who does not passionately believe in the perfectibility of man, has no dedication nor any membership in literature," Steinbeck said.

"Having taken God-like power, we must seek in ourselves the responsibility and wisdom we once prayed some deity might have. Man himself has become our greatest hazard and our only hope," he said.

In his 1962 Nobel Prize acceptance speech, Steinbeck said, "The ancient commission of the writer has not changed. He is charged with exposing our many grievous faults and failures, with dredging up to light our dark and dangerous dreams for the purpose of improvement."

Steinbeck was born in Salinas, California, in 1902. He attended Stanford University, but did not graduate. He went to New York, where he worked as a reporter and as a laborer. His first book, *Cup of Gold*, was published in 1929. He returned to California, where he spent most of his time writing and working at menial jobs.

He died in 1968 in New York.

Benjamin Spock (1903–)
The Common Sense Book of Baby and Child Care, 1946

41

"I want to talk to parents as if they are sensible people."

THE TIMES: President Franklin Roosevelt died. Hiroshima and Nagasaki, Japan, were destroyed by atomic bombs. John Hersey won a Pulitzer Prize for his war novel *A Bell for Adano*. Robert Penn Warren published his most famous novel, *All the King's Men*, based on the life of southern political boss Huey Long. World War II ended with the defeat of Germany in Europe and Japan in the Pacific. The Atomic Energy Commission was created. Ranch-style houses were in vogue.

"You know more than you think you do."

With these reassuring words, Dr. Benjamin Spock began one of the most successful and influential books in the history of American publishing. Spock's *Common Sense Book of Baby and Child Care*, published in 1946, sold 750,000 copies within the first year. Since its publication, it has sold more than 24 million copies in America, outselling every book besides the Bible. Now, in its sixth edition, it has sold more than 40 million copies worldwide and has been translated into sixteen languages. The book has influenced generations of parents and children and altered forever the worldwide approach to child-rearing.

The ninety-year-old Spock, who resides in the British Virgin Islands, was a struggling pediatrician in New York City when Pocket Books approached him in 1943 to write a manual for parents on child care. According to Spock, the editors at Pocket Books were looking for a children's doctor who knew something about Freudian concepts and how they could relate to child-rearing techniques. At the time, Spock was the only pediatrician who had been professionally trained in Freudian psychoanalysis. He had spent five years training at the New York Psychoanalytic Institute following his pediatrics training. According to Spock, "no book existed which combined sound pediatrics and sound psychology."

He wrote the book based on his own experiences as a pediatrician and the experiences of his patients and their parents. He sent copies of his completed manuscript to several physicians, teachers, and parents for their suggestions — some of which he incorporated into the final draft of the book.

Pocket Books contracted only for a paperback edition of Spock's book, claiming it could sell more copies at the reduced paperback price.

"I was glad that the book's low price would make my views available to as many people as possible," Spock said. But he was troubled that libraries did not stock paperbacks and that book reviewers seldom reviewed them. He wanted the book to have the widest coverage available. So Spock contracted with Duell, Sloan and Pearce to publish a hardcover edition simultaneously.

Having a paperback and hardcover edition appear at the same time was an unheard-of publishing practice. It turned out to be a stroke of pure publishing genius.

When the book came out, the paperback version outsold the hardcover by more than 500,000 copies to just under 6,500 copies. But Spock earned more on the hardcover sales than the paperback. He never received an advance from Pocket Books.

". . . I wasn't averse to earning money from the book, but without an advance, the initial royalty . . . would only add up to $1,500 a year if the book sold 200,000 copies a year," Spock said. Spock's ultimate earnings from the sale of the book are in the millions of dollars.

The book was nearly twice as long as the publisher wanted, and Spock was two years late in completing it. As new subjects came to mind, Spock added them to the book. He wanted drawings to illustrate sections of the book. They were provided by the artist Dorothea Fox. Throughout the life of the book, the original illustrations by Fox have remained intact, except for a few minor changes to accommodate changing technology.

The book told parents everything they needed to know about raising children and became considered by most parents as the "baby bible."

Spock advocated love and understanding when it came to child rearing.

"Every baby needs to be smiled at, talked to, fondled gently and lovingly. . . ." he wrote.

Spock did not adhere to the old-fashioned regimented methods of child rearing. His advice to parents went against the grain of what most child-development experts of the times advocated, among them noted children's expert Dr. John Watson, who insisted that "kissing and coddling infants is taboo."

Spock also wanted to reassure parents. "No parent is going to do a perfect job. Don't feel guilty; you are probably doing the best job you can. Don't be too dependent on child-guidance experts. . . ." he wrote.

Spock also did not include a litany of specific tasks children should accomplish at certain ages.

"More than nine out of ten babies who are distinctly slow in motion development turn out to have normal intelligence," Spock assured worried parents.

He addressed almost every question a parent might need answered, dealing with the psychological as well as physical needs of the child.

Despite the enormous success of the book, Spock worried about its impact.

"I was scared that the book would be misunderstood, that somebody thinking she was following my advice, would do something that would make a child worse," he said.

Spock fell out of favor with parents when he became an outspoken critic of the Vietnam War during the 1960s. In 1968, he was convicted by the U.S. government for his anti-draft activities, including the burning of draft cards. The conviction was overturned a year later.

Despite his controversial stands during the war, Spock's book continued to sell, in part because he was viewed as a true advocate of loving relationships between children and parents.

"A child is born with a greater capacity to love than hate, to build than to destroy, to profit from every chance to learn and mature," he said.

Spock was born in 1903 in New Haven, Connecticut, attended Yale University, and received his medical degree from Columbia University.

42 Rachel Carson (1907–64)
The Silent Spring, 1962

"She created a tide of environmental consciousness that has not ebbed."

THE TIMES: John F. Kennedy was president. *Tropic of Cancer*, the controversial book by Henry Miller, banned since 1934, became available in America. Joseph Heller published his most popular book, *Catch 22*. *To Kill a Mockingbird*, written by Harper Lee, won a Pulitzer Prize. President Kennedy announced his plan for the Peace Corps. Television is called "a vast wasteland," by the chairman of the FCC, Newton Minow. Alan Shepard was the first American in space. Roger Maris, of the New York Yankees, beat Babe Ruth's home-run record by hitting sixty-one home runs. American author and Nobel Prize winner Ernest Hemingway committed suicide. The Cuban Missile Crisis began.

Rachel Carson's influential and controversial book *The Silent Spring*, published in 1962, drew immediate attacks from the agricultural chemical industry, which spent more money trying to ridicule both the book and its author than it did on cleaning up the environmental mess it had created. "[T]he book's major

*   *   *

Nader was born in 1934 in Winsted, Connecticut, and attended the Woodrow Wilson School of Public and International Affairs at Princeton University, from which he graduated in 1955. He attended Harvard Law School, where he served as an editor of *The Harvard Law Record*. He graduated in 1958 and set up law practice in Hartford, Connecticut. He served briefly as a free-lance writer for *Atlantic Monthly* and *The Christian Science Monitor*.

In 1958, Nader published his first article on automobile safety, "American Cars: Designed for Death," which was published in *The Harvard Law Record*. It served as a precursor to his most famous and influential work, *Unsafe at Any Speed*.

James Coleman (1926–)

48 Equality of Educational Opportunity, 1966

"[Integration] is the most consistent mechanism for improving the quality of education of disadvantaged children."

THE TIMES: Nearly four hundred thousand troops were committed to the war in Vietnam — American casualties reached nearly 7,000 killed and approximately 38,000 wounded. The U.S. Supreme Court issued the "Miranda ruling," requiring police to read suspects their rights. Truman Capote published *In Cold Blood*. The old Metropolitan Opera House was demolished. The word "psychedelic," describing hallucinatory drugs such as LSD, came into popular use. Bell-bottom pants were in vogue for young men and women. The American population reached 200 million people.

A former chemist, James Coleman, is responsible for writing the report that helped mix black and white children within American schools.

In 1965, Coleman was appointed to act as codirector of an comprehensive national survey on educational opportunities for minority groups in America. The report, *Equality of Educational Opportunity*, published in 1966 by the U.S. Government

Printing Office, is considered a landmark in American education. It helped President Richard Nixon in establishing his education policies for the country.

Coleman, who was born in 1926 in Bedford, Indiana, entered the navy in 1944. After being discharged from the service, he studied at Indiana University and later Purdue University, where he received a degree in chemical engineering in 1949. Coleman served as a chemist with the Eastman Kodak Company in Rochester, New York.

According to a *New York Times* profile published in 1970, Coleman always had, "a deep concern throughout life for a democratic, pluralistic society."

He went to Columbia University, where he obtained his Ph.D. in sociology in 1955. He joined the faculty of Johns Hopkins University in 1959, where he served as an associate professor and professor of social relations.

The 1964 Civil Rights Act included provisions to conduct a study, and report to the president and Congress on the issue of equal educational opportunities in American public schools. Coleman was appointed by the secretary of the United States Office of Education to conduct the survey.

In the fall of 1965, Coleman began the extensive study. It cost $1.5 million to complete. Coleman's study surveyed educational opportunities available to blacks and other minorities along with disadvantaged whites. It involved the study of nearly four thousand schools throughout America, thousands of teachers and school officials, and nearly six hundred thousand students from the first to the twelfth grade. Coleman used achievement tests to measure the cultural skills considered important for social and economic success. In July 1966, Coleman presented his 737-page report to the president and Congress.

Coleman's report showed that de facto segregation was

widespread throughout the country, and that the quality of education for blacks and other minorities was inferior. According to Coleman, few black Americans attended college, and twice as many blacks as whites dropped out of school.

Black schools were overcrowded and run-down compared to white schools, Coleman explained, and teachers in the poorer black schools in the country had less academic ability than teachers in more prosperous predominantly white areas of the country.

Coleman maintained that putting more money into existing black schools would have little impact on black students. Instead, Coleman argued that equality in public education could be achieved if blacks and other minorities were sent to middle-class white schools. Minority students, according to Coleman, could increase their educational capacity by enrolling in predominantly middle-class white schools. White middle-class students, he explained, would not suffer any educational loss from associating with poorer minority students.

Coleman published an article in 1966 in *Public Interest* in which he argued that the social and educational backgrounds of teachers and students, rather than the physical makeup of the schools, were the key factors in a school's success. He maintained that integration was beneficial to minority students in a predominantly middle-class environment. He also maintained that minority students needed to feel they were a part of American society, not apart from it, and that a sense of personal pride should be encouraged. According to Coleman, development and encouragement of black pride would "have more effect on Negro achievement than any other single factor . . . not because of the changes they will create in the white community but principally because of the changes they create in the Negro himself."

Although Coleman's report was soundly criticized by many prominent white and black leaders, an analysis by educational scholars showed that Coleman's study was accurate.

In March 1970, President Richard Nixon delivered a special report on education reform in America in which he endorsed Coleman's recommendations. Nixon announced that the government planned to allocate $1.5 billion for 1971 and 1972 to help school districts in America eliminate racial segregation in public schools. Coleman was appointed as a special adviser to Nixon's desegregation plan. The plan was attacked by the NAACP, which filed suit in federal court on the grounds that it failed to achieve true racial equality.

Coleman hailed Nixon's actions as "the first time there has been a positive commitment, supported by resources, to creating strong and stable school integration."

By the middle of the 1970s, Coleman found little to praise about the progress of public-school integration. Court-ordered busing to achieve integration, he explained, had accelerated the flight of middle-class whites to the suburbs. According to Coleman, despite the government's best efforts, the prospect of improved educational opportunities for black children was declining.

49 Paul Ehrlich (1932–)
The Population Bomb, 1968

"If population control measures are not initiated immediately, and effectively, all the technology man can bring to bear will not fend off the misery to come."

THE TIMES: The first football Super Bowl was held. The North Vietnamese Tet Offensive caught American forces off guard. Although the enemy forces suffered massive losses, the Tet offensive further fueled antiwar protests in America. President Lyndon Johnson announced he would not run for reelection. Martin Luther King, Jr., was assassinated in Memphis, Tennessee. Senator Robert Kennedy was assassinated in Los Angeles, California, during his presidential campaign. The war in Vietnam was the longest war in American history. Norman Mailer published *The Armies of the Night*, for which he won a Pulitzer Prize. Richard Nixon was elected president.

The 1968 best-seller *The Population Bomb*, written by entomologist and author Paul Ehrlich, accurately predicted the massive worldwide famines of the 1970s and 1980s. Despite Ehrlich's dire warnings that worldwide starvation was inevitable unless nations were willing to limit population growth, the issue of population control has yet to be addressed in an effective way.

Ehrlich maintained that all human beings had certain "inalienable rights," including the right to drink pure water and eat; the right to live in an uncrowded world; the right to live in a world free from environmental poisons; and the right to be free from the threat of nuclear war.

"Too many cars, too many factories, too much detergent, too much pesticide . . . too little water, too much carbon dioxide — all can be traced easily to too many people," Ehrlich wrote.

According to Ehrlich, the largest rates of population growth were among undeveloped countries, including most African and Asian countries and many Latin American ones. These countries were not industrialized and had problems growing food. He maintained that the world population would continue to grow as long as the birthrate exceeded the death rate.

"Medical science . . . has been able to depress the death rate . . . and at the same time increase the birth rate; healthier people have more babies," he wrote.

According to Ehrlich, the population has been growing faster than the world's ability to produce food — even in such industrialized nations as America and Japan. Seventy-five percent of the people in the world went to bed hungry, and between 10 and 20 million people starved to death each year, according to Ehrlich. A United Nations report estimated that by 1998, the world population would increase to 6 billion people — a projected growth of 97 million people a year, the highest ever in history. According to Ehrlich's *The Population Bomb*, mankind will starve to death unless population growth is limited.

"Family planning is a disaster because it is giving people a false sense of security," he said, maintaining that no one should have more than two children.

"[A]nything beyond that is irresponsible, suicidal," he said.

Ehrlich maintained that America should discourage population growth by imposing severe taxes on such items as baby food and diapers. He also advocated for America to take a lead role in limiting world population growth by making population control a condition for America's food-aid programs. He maintained that America should stop sending food to such countries as India, where "dispassionate analysis indicates that the unbalance between food and population is hopeless."

Ehrlich noted that when family planning began in India, its population was more than 350 million, but that it had grown to 500 million during the course of the family planning program.

Ehrlich outlined four steps that needed to be taken to control population growth. He called for tax laws aimed at discouraging reproduction; creation of a federal commission charged with educating the public to the dangers of overpopulation; increased federal support for research in the environmental and behavioral sciences; and mandatory birth-control education in public schools and the abolition of laws against abortions.

"No action that we can take at this late date can prevent a great deal of future misery from starvation and environmental deterioration," he explained.

"The dimensions of the programs that must be mounted if we are to survive are awe inspiring," he said.

"If I'm right, we will save the world. If I'm wrong, people will still be better fed, better housed, and happier, thanks to our efforts," he added.

Ehrlich wrote *The Population Bomb* at the urging of the conservation organization the Sierra Club. It was published by

Sierra Club Ballantine books in 1968, and within two years sold one million copies. It received the Best-sellers Paperback of the Year Award in 1970.

Following publication of the book, Ehrlich appeared on *The Tonight Show*, where Johnny Carson interviewed him for a full hour. His appearance on the television show drew a record number of responses. Ehrlich began receiving upward of twenty-five letters a day following the publication of the book.

Ehrlich was born in Philadelphia, Pennsylvania, in 1932. He attended the University of Pennsylvania and received his Ph.D. in 1957 from the University of Kansas. He teaches at Stanford University.

He is the author of numerous scientific papers, articles, and books. He is also the founder and president of Zero Population Growth, Inc., a political action organization aimed at accomplishing many of the goals set forth in *The Population Bomb*.

"We are today involved in the events leading to famine; tomorrow we may be destroyed by its consequences. . . . I'm no hero. This is just a survival reaction. I'm running for my life," Ehrlich said.

50 Daniel Ellsberg, (1931–   )
The Pentagon Papers, 1971

"It's like the defrocking of the Wizard of Oz."

THE TIMES: Lieutenant William Calley was convicted of murder for his role in the massacre of men, women, and children in the South Vietnamese village of My Lai. The voting age was lowered to eighteen. Dee Brown published *Bury My Heart at Wounded Knee*, the story of the systematic annihilation of the American Indians. The Supreme Court overturned the 1967 draft-evasion conviction against former world boxing champion Muhammad Ali. The largest rock-and-roll festival in the world was held in Woodstock, New York. Washington, D.C. police arrested five men, charging them with breaking into the Democratic party headquarters in the Watergate apartment complex. Richard Nixon was reelected president.

Daniel Ellsberg, an ex–U.S. Marine sharp-shooter, shot directly from the hip when, in 1971, he released the forty-seven-volume secret Pentagon study of America's involvement in the Vietnam War to *The New York Times*. His actions led to a classic confrontation in the courts between the government's right to keep its activities secret in the name of national security and the media's right to keep the public informed. The publication of the Pentagon Papers in the *Times* and other newspapers throughout the country showed clearly that the American government had deceived the American people about the war in Vietnam. This ultimately led to widespread protest against the war and the government's handling of it.

"If I am found guilty and the act of leaking thereby becomes a crime . . . we'll have a censorship system that's airtight — a government press," Ellsberg said.

A former Pentagon analyst and ardent supporter of the war, Ellsberg had become so concerned about his involvement in the continuation of the Vietnam War that he secretly released the Pentagon Papers to the media. The secret papers included four thousand pages of documents. Three thousand pages of analysis, and 2.5 million words — all classified as secret, top secret, or top secret–sensitive.

The papers first appeared in *The New York Times* and *The Washington Post*. The *Times* began publishing front-page articles based on the Pentagon Papers, including excerpts, in a Sunday edition in June 1971. After three installments, the government obtained an injunction preventing further publication. However, by then *The Washington Post*, *The Boston Globe*, and other newspapers began covering the story.

The government case against the newspapers was decided in favor of the *Times* and the *Post* by the Supreme Court, and publication of the controversial Pentagon Papers continued.

In 1967, Ellsberg was one of thirty-five researchers assigned to help compile a history of American and Vietnamese relations from 1945 through 1967. The project was undertaken by Secretary of Defense Robert McNamara, who was disillusioned by the futility of the war and wanted future historians to be able to determine what had gone wrong. For more than a year, Ellsberg and the other researchers worked on the papers.

According to Ellsberg, during this time he revised his opinion of presidential responsibility for the policy of military escalation.

"I think now to a large extent it was an American president's war," he said. "No American president, Republican or Democrat, wanted to be the president who lost the war or who lost Saigon."

He concluded that the Vietnam War had been an "American war almost from its beginning." The government denied the theory that the war was a Vietnamese civil war.

"In practical terms, it has been . . . a war of Vietnamese — not all of them but enough to persist — against American policy and American financing, proxies, technicians, firepower, and finally, troops and pilots," Ellsberg wrote.

"To call a conflict in which one army is financed and equipped entirely by foreigners a 'civil war' simply screens a more painful reality: that the war is, after all, a foreign aggression. Our aggression," he explained.

Ellsberg was identified as the person who released the Pentagon Papers to the media, and he was indicted on two counts of converting government property to personal use and of illegally possessing government documents. New indictments were added, including twelve criminal charges of conspiracy, theft, and violation of the Espionage Act.

According to Ellsberg, he was "willing to go to prison to help end this war."

His first trial was declared a mistrial in 1972. His lawyers argued that the Pentagon Papers were in the public domain and did not constitute a threat to national security.

In 1973, as the case was about to go to trial for the second time, all charges against Ellsberg were dismissed. The judge cited government misconduct, including illegal wiretapping and a break-in at the office of Ellsberg's former psychiatrist. The judge declared that Ellsberg and the American people had been "victims of a conspiracy to deprive us of our civil liberties."

The shocking revelations contained in the Pentagon Papers regarding the secrecy with which the government had acted and the attack on the freedom of the press by the government all led to extreme scrutiny of the executive branch of government.

"The demystification and desanctification of the president has begun," Ellsberg said at his trial. "It's like the defrocking of the Wizard of Oz."

Ellsberg was born in Chicago, Illinois, in 1931. He attended Harvard University, where he earned a Ph.D. in economics. He served for two years in the U.S. Marines in 1954, and he joined the Rand Corporation in 1959. In 1964, he joined the staff of the assistant secretary of defense, where he argued in favor of President Johnson's Vietnam War policies.

In his own book, *Papers on the War*, published in 1972, Ellsberg projected that the Vietnam War would be "[a] continued conflict, at increasing levels of violence, followed some day — probably later rather than sooner, and after more and more deaths, costs, destruction, and dissension at home — by U.S. withdrawal. . . ."

Ellsberg contacted editors, passed along information to government committees, leaders, and elected officials, expressing his concerns about the war. He ultimately resigned from the Rand Corporation and accepted a post as a senior research associate at the Massachusetts Institute of Technology's Center for International Studies.

According to Ellsberg, he was frustrated by his failure to influence American policy and upset over the continued escalation of the war. It was at this point that he brought the Pentagon Papers to the attention of the media.

"I think that what might be at stake if this involvement goes on is a change in our society as radical and ominous as could be brought about by our occupation by a foreign power," Ellsberg said.

On April 30, 1975, the last Americans were airlifted out of Saigon. The longest war in American history was finally over.

Suggested Reading

Amerigo Vespucci (1454–1512)
   Cahoon, Herbert. *America from Amerigo Vespucci to the Louisiana Purchase* (1976).
   Lester, C. Edwards. *The Life and Voyages of Americus Vespucci* (1903).

Stephen Day (c. 1594–1668)
   Kimber, Sidney A. *The Story of an Old Press* (1990).

Benjamin Franklin (1706–90)
   Clark, Ronald. *Benjamin Franklin: A Biography* (1989).
   Cohen, Bernard. *Benjamin Franklin's Science* (1990).
   Van Doren, Carl. *Benjamin Franklin (1991).*

Thomas Paine (1737–1809)
   Conway, Moncure. *Life of Thomas Paine* (1892).
   Cheetham, John. *The Life of Thomas Paine* (1989).
   Fast, Howard. *Citizen Tom Paine* (1987).

Thomas Jefferson (1743–1826)
Boorstin, Daniel. *The Lost World of Thomas Jefferson* (1960).
Brodie, Fawn McKay. *Thomas Jefferson: An Intimate Biography* (1974).
Cunningham, Noble. *In Pursuit of Reason: The Life of Thomas Jefferson*, (1977).

Noah Webster (1758–1843)
Rollins, Richard. *The Long Journey of Noah Webster* (1980).
Shoemaker, Ervin. *Noah Webster: Pioneer of Learning* (1936).
Warfel, Harry. *Noah Webster: School Master to America* (1966).

Alexander Hamilton (1755–1804), James Madison (1751–1836), John Jay (1745–1829)
Morris, Richard. *Witness at the Creation: Hamilton, Madison, Jay and the Constitution* (1985).

Charles Brockden Brown (1771–1810)
Allen, Paul. *The Life of Charles Brockden Brown* (1975).
Clark, David. *Charles Brockden Brown: Pioneer Voice of America* (1952).
Dunlap, William. *The Life of Charles Brockden Brown* (1988).

Francis Scott Key (1779–1843)
Patterson, Lillie. *Francis Scott Key: Poet and Patriot* (1991).
Silkett, John. *Francis Scott Key and the History of the Star Spangled Banner* (1978).
Weybright, Victor. *Spangled Banner* (1975).

James Kent (1763–1847)
Kent, William. *Memoirs and Letters of James Kent* (1898).

Horton, John. *James Kent: A Study in Conservativism 1763–1847* (1983).

William McGuffey (1800–73).
Culbertson, Marjorie Grace. *The McGuffey Readers and Their Influence on Modern Education and Readers* (1959).
Scully, James. *A Biography of William McGuffey* (1988).
Vail, Henry. *A History of the McGuffey Readers* (1970).

Ralph Waldo Emerson (1803–82)
Barish, Evelyn. *Emerson: The Roots of Prophecy* (1990).
Bosco, Ronald, and Albert Von Frank, eds. *The Complete Sermons of Ralph Waldo Emerson* (1991).
Reaver, Russell. *Emerson As Myth Maker* (1954).
Tilton, Eleanor, ed. *The Letters of Ralph Waldo Emerson* (1991).

Richard Dana (1815–82)
Gale, Robert. *Richard Henry Dana, Jr.* (1969).
Hyams, Norman. *Richard Henry Dana in California* (1950).
Shapiro, Samuel. *Richard Henry Dana, Jr.* (1961).

Margaret Fuller (1810–50)
Allen, Margaret. *The Achievement of Margaret Fuller* (1979).
Blanchard, Paula. *Margaret Fuller: From Transcendentalism to Revolution* (1987).
Stern, Madeline. *The Life of Margaret Fuller* (1991).

Frederick Douglass (1817–95)
Blight, David. *Frederick Douglass' Civil War* (1991).
Douglass, Frederick. *The Frederick Douglass Papers: Speeches, Debates and Interviews* (1986).

Higgins, Nathan. *Slave and Citizen: The Life of Frederick Douglass* (1987).

Henry David Thoreau (1817–62)
Harding, Walter. *Henry David Thoreau: A Profile* (1971).
Hough, Henry Beetle. *Thoreau of Walden: The Man and His Eventful Life* (1970).
Krutch, Joseph. *Henry David Thoreau* (1974).

Harriet Beecher Stowe (1811–96)
Adams, John. *Harriet Beecher Stowe* (1963).
Crozier, Alice. *The Novels of Harriet Beecher Stowe* (1969).
Moers, Ellen. *Harriet Beecher Stowe and American Literature* (1978).

Abraham Lincoln (1809–65)
Catton, Bruce. *Two Roads to Sumter* (1963).
Mitgang, Herbert. *The Fiery Trial: A Life of Lincoln* (1974).
Oates, Stephen. *With Malice Toward None: The Life of Abraham Lincoln* (1977).
Sandburg, Carl. *Abraham Lincoln: The War Years* (1939).

Elizabeth Peabody (1804–94)
Fisher, Hersha. *The Education of Elizabeth Peabody* (1981).
Henderson, Darwin. *Elizabeth Peabody and Lucy Gage* (1976).
Tharp, Louise. *The Peabody Sisters of Salem* (1950).

Henry George (1839–97)
De Mille, Anna. *Henry George: Citizen of the World* (1950).
Rather, Lois. *Henry George: Printer to Author* (1978).
Thomas, John. *Alternative America* (1983).

Helen Hunt Jackson (1831–85)
  Friend, Ruth. *Helen Hunt Jackson: A Critical Study* (1985).
  Mathes, Valerie. *Friends of the California Mission Indians: Helen Hunt Jackson and Her Legacy* (1988).
  Odell, Ruth. *Helen Hunt Jackson* (1939).

Emma Lazarus (1849–87)
  Cowan, Paul. *The Poet of Liberty* (1986).
  Lefer, Diane. *Emma Lazarus* (1988).
  Levinson, Nancy. *I Lift My Lamp: Emma Lazarus and the Statue of Liberty* (1986).

Edward Bellamy (1850–98)
  Bowman, Sylvia. *Edward Bellamy* (1986).
  Michaelis, Richard. *Looking Further Forward: An Answer to Looking Backward* (1971).
  Morgan, Arthur. *The Philosophy of Edward Bellamy* (1945).

Andrew Carnegie (1835–1919)
  Harlow, Alvin. *Andrew Carnegie* (1953).
  Hughes, Jonathan. *The Vital Few* (1966).
  Winkler, John. *Incredible Carnegie* (1931).

Jacob Riis (1849–1914)
  Carlson, Kathryn. *The Photographer as Educator* (1981).
  Fried, Lewis. *Makers of the City* (1990).
  Ware, Louise. *Jacob Riis* (1983).

Alfred Mahan (1840–1914)
  Dingman, Roger. *Japan and Mahan* (1990).
  Leslie, Reo. *The Religion of Alfred Thayer Mahan* (1990).
  Puleston, William. *Mahan* (1939).

Susan B. Anthony (1820–1906)
Harper, Ida. *The Life and Work of Susan B. Anthony* (1908).
Lutz, Alma. *Susan B. Anthony: Rebel, Crusader, Humanitarian* (1959).

Stephen Crane (1871–1900)
Beer, Thomas. *Stephen Crane: A Study in American Letters* (1923).
Follett, Wilson, ed. *The Works of Stephen Crane* (1926).
Trent, William, et al., eds. *The Cambridge History of American Literature* (1933).

Henry Demarest Lloyd (1847–1903)
Digby-Junger, Richard. *The Gilded Age Journalist as Advocate* (1991).
Linerman, Paul. *Reform Tendencies of Henry Demarest Lloyd* (1931).
Lloyd, Caroline. *Henry Demarest Lloyd: A Biography* (1912).

Fannie Farmer (1857–1915)
Smallzried, Kathleen Ann. *The Everlasting Pleasure* (1956).

Edwin Markham (1852–1940)
Hampton, Vernon. *The Meaning and Influence of Markham's "The Man With the Hoe"* (1987).
Reid, Francis. *Poet Edwin Markham* (1940).
Stidger, William. *Edwin Markham* (1983).

Theodore Dreiser (1871–1945)
Mukherjee, Arun. *The Gospel of Wealth in the American Novel* (1987).
Riggio, Thomas. *Dreiser-Mencken Letters* (1986).

Antiope too might be in danger should the fight get out of hand. She wondered briefly where Molpadia's pair Amazon might be.

Antiope refused to budge. "I'm going to watch," she insisted. "Watch and learn, you said."

Molpadia suddenly attacked again, and the shafts of the two spears cracked against each other several times before the two girls became locked together, neither one giving ground. But Molpadia was older and bigger and stronger, and gradually she forced her spear point down toward Hippolyta's face.

If she bloods me, I will not cry out, Hippolyta told herself. *I will not.* She could feel the heat of Molpadia's breath on her brow.

All of a sudden Hippolyta shifted her weight, throwing her opponent off-balance. She took a chance and whipped the butt of her spear up to give the older girl a crack on the head.

Molpadia reeled back with a curse, but before Hippolyta could follow up with the spearpoint, Antiope let out a shrill, awful scream.

Hippolyta twisted around and saw a mountain cat emerging from the undergrowth, a great bloody slash on its right flank still oozing blood. Its eyes were fixed on Antiope, and a vicious growl rumbled in its throat.

Antiope didn't shrink before the great cat, but her little spear was shaking in her hands. The animal was bigger than she, and only a few short yards separated them.

Hippolyta realized that the wounded cat must be crazed with pain. It was ready to spring.

As the cat leaped, Hippolyta threw herself forward, knocking Antiope off her feet. Thrusting her spear upward, Hippolyta rammed the point deep into the animal's tawny breast.

Hot blood showered down, nearly blinding her, and instinctively she pushed the spear and cat away, to keep the flailing claws from raking her face.

The cat thudded onto its side, a low growl rattled in its throat, and then it was dead.

Molpadia pointed at a wound in the cat's flank. "I did that."

"Yes, but you didn't finish the job, Molpadia. You were too slow," Hippolyta said, standing. She was amazed that her legs could still hold her, for now that the danger was passed, they were suddenly shaking with terror. She ignored her trembling legs and wrenched the spear from the cat's body.

Taking a deep breath, she hefted the cat onto her shoulders, caring nothing for the blood that trickled down her arm. The golden hide would make a fine tunic or a warm lining for a winter cloak. The cat's teeth she'd turn into a necklace for Antiope, who had stood so bravely, armed only with her little toy spear.

"Keep the bird, Molpadia," Hippolyta said with a grin of triumph. "I have a better prize now." She handed her spear to Antiope. "Here, sister, if you carry this for me, we'll head for home. Two hunters together."

Antiope took the spear, and it was so much larger than her own she had to wrap both arms around it. But she didn't complain. Her grin practically swallowed her face.

Molpadia followed silently behind, the partridge slung over her shoulder.

They were within sight of the tethered mare when another horse came galloping through the trees.

Molpadia had already snatched up her bow and arrow, ready to fire, but the rider was no enemy from Phrygia or Lycia. It was Aella, one of the queen's royal guards.

"Hippolyta, thank the goddess I have found you," Aella called, waving an arm. "You and Antiope must return at once to the palace."

"What is it? What has happened?" Hippolyta cried out.

But message delivered, Aella had already turned and was riding back the way she'd come.

Antiope stood trembling, arms around the spear. "Is Mother all right, Hippolyta? Is—"

Without answering, Hippolyta threw the cat to the ground. She grabbed the spear from her little sister, then dragged her to the horse. Untying the mount, Hippolyta leaped onto its bare back, then leaned down. "To me!" she cried.

Antiope reached up and was yanked onto the horse's

back, behind Hippolyta. Fastening her arms around her sister's waist, she nestled her head into the small of Hippolyta's back.

"Ready," she cried.

Then they were off at a gallop toward Themiscyra, the royal capital, as fast as their hardy little mountain pony could go.

CHAPTER TWO

THE QUEEN

All Hippolyta could see of Aella was the dust her horse had kicked up speeding back home.

She turned and looked behind her. Almost at the edge of sight were Molpadia and, farther behind her, another figure, presumably the girl Molpadia had been hunting with.

"Will we get there soon? Will Mother be all right? Will . . ." Antiope's questions filled Hippolyta's ears.

"I know nothing," Hippolyta called over her shoulder. "No more than you do. Now be quiet."

Soon the gleam of the River Thermodon was visible ahead, like a long, shiny-skinned adder winding its way north to the dark waters of the Euxine Sea.

On the banks of the river stood the capital of Themiscyra, a quiet settlement of wooden lodges, cabins, and storehouses that had the slightly ramshackle air of a temporary encampment. Hippolyta knew that long ago the Amazons, like their Scythian ancestors, had traveled from place to place, living off the land. But finally they had settled here, close to the running waters.

To Hippolyta, however, Themiscyra was home, the only place she wanted to be.

As soon as she and Antiope dismounted and led the pony through the gate of the wooden palisade and past a row of merchants' stalls, she could hear the buzz of voices filling the street. It was not the usual, happy sound of women at work. Hippolyta was sure it was like the sharp *pick-buzz* of angry insects. She couldn't quite make out what people were saying.

About halfway into the city, they came upon a knot of women debating vigorously and clogging the way.

"Not another?" one gray-haired merchant was saying.

"It's the will of Artemis," answered another.

"What's to be done? What's to be done?" The same question was suddenly in a dozen mouths.

"The queen will know" came the answer from a weaver, her hands full of cloth. "She will do what is right."

"What is right? Or what is best?" That was the merchant.

"I trust the queen," the weaver said again.

Hippolyta pushed them aside. "Let us through."

But when the merchant cried to her, "What says Queen Otrere, princess? What says your mother?" Hippolyta glared at her.

"We know nothing," she answered. "Nor can we find out if you don't let us go to her."

Silently the women made a path for the two girls, and about fifty feet farther in, they reached the courtyard of the royal palace.

Like the other buildings, it was built of wood but reinforced with slate and sandstone. Normally Hippolyta's heart lifted whenever she came home. But this time it was as if a heavy gray mist hung over the turreted roof.

Hippolyta gratefully handed a servant girl the pony's reins, and her weapons as well. Then she and Antiope went over to Aella. "What is it?" Hippolyta asked. "What's happened?"

"Hush," Aella said. "We can't speak of it here. Inside, quickly. But don't run. Walk like princesses. Like Amazons. Heads high. Show no fear. You are daughters of Otrere."

Hippolyta squared her shoulders and saw out of the corner of her eye that her little sister did the same. Then, following Aella, they went into the palace, into a danger they did not yet understand.

The mood inside the palace was subdued, as if everyone was afraid to speak openly. Aella led them straight to the queen's bedchamber. A pair of armed guards, black hair bound up in warrior's knots, flanked the closed door.

"Asteria? Philippis?" Antiope said, but they didn't answer, and that was odd because she was a great favorite with the guards.

"Come," Hippolyta said, taking her by the hand.

Silently the guards opened the doors, and they went in.

Queen Otrere was propped up in her bed. The old priestess Demonassa, who also acted as a midwife, was standing at the bedside in long gray robes that were now stained with birth blood. Seated at the bed foot was Hippolyta's younger sister Melanippe, who was just two years older than little Antiope.

Melanippe looked up and sighed. "Thank the goddess you're here, sisters." She stood and came over to them. "When I sent for Orithya, she refused to come."

"*Orithya.*" Hippolyta spoke her older sister's name as if it burned her mouth. These days Orithya spent more time with the warrior queen Valasca, who commanded the army in times of war, than she did with her own mother. Hippolyta was furious with Orithya. Family should come first.

"That Orithya would not answer your call is no surprise." Hippolyta added, "I no longer consider her a sister. The blood runs thin in her. She belongs to Valasca just as if she came shooting out between that old hawk's legs fully armored."

Antiope spotted her mother and saw what she was holding in her arms—unbound and naked. Rushing forward with a great grin, Antiope cried out, "The baby! She's here at last."

"The baby," Hippolyta said, looking over at the bed. Suddenly she realized what all the people outside had been talking about. The child hadn't been swaddled yet, and even from this far away, she could see it was a boy, the second such her mother had borne. The first had been nine years earlier, right after Melanippe, a year before Antiope.

Hippolyta remembered that day well. She'd been four years old, which was old enough to love the infant and old enough to understand that it could never remain in Themiscyra. Boys were not welcome in Amazon society, and they were given away to passing strangers. Except for the firstborn boy born to a queen: He was always returned to his father.

But not the second.

Hippolyta knew Amazon history. Every girl her age

was well versed in it: Long ago in the city of Arimaspa, the Amazon women had been part of the Scythian race. They'd lived with men and cared for their sons. But a pair of arrogant princes had brought ruin to the people by stealing gold belonging to the gods. In turn the gods rained destruction down on Arimaspa.

The goddess Artemis had saved them, leading the women away from that cursed place one moonless night. They spent years looking for the right place to establish a community of women, free of all kings, princes, and husbands, a community dedicated to the goddess.

Artemis decreed that all sons born to the women from then on were to be sent away before their first birthdays. However, there was a special rule for the Amazon queens. They would be allowed only one live son, for it had been foretold by Artemis' brother, the god Apollo, that if a second son born to a queen were allowed to grow to manhood, he would be the cause of the death of the Amazon race. It was why the priestesses and midwives supplied the queens with special herbs and potions that almost always guaranteed a girl child.

Almost.

But not always.

Antiope was playing with the baby's little fingers and singing softly to him, oblivious.

"You know what this means?" Melanippe whispered, twisting a finger through her brown curls.

Hippolyta nodded. Then she went over to the bed and took her mother's weakly offered hand. "I'm so sorry, Mother," she said, her voice tearing as if on a splinter of wood. "I know how hard this will be on you."

There was a spark of determination in Otrere's eyes, a spark that lent strength to her pale face. Her voice was amazingly firm. "I can't do what is expected, Hippolyta," she said. "Not having carried this child below my heart. You must be prepared for the worst."

Confused, Hippolyta let her mother's hand drop. "I don't understand. What do you mean, you *can't* do it? Artemis requires it. A second son *must* be sacrificed upon Artemis' altar. It's the price we pay for the goddess's protection. It's our pact with her. In this life an Amazon does what she must. How often have you told me so?"

For a moment Otrere's face went pale. Old Demonassa started forward, but the queen sat up, color rushing back into her cheeks. She waved Demonassa away.

"I can't sacrifice the child, daughter. I have felt him like a hammer beneath my breast," Otrere said. "He kicked with such life. I cannot believe the goddess would have me snuff out such a fighter."

"But—" Hippolyta took a deep breath and tried to frame her response carefully. She might not get another chance. "If you *don't* do this thing, there will be awful consequences. To you. To the child. To *all* your children." She waved her hand around the room, taking in her sisters as well as the guards and the priestess.

For a moment Otrere glanced down at the little boy in her arms, and her brown eyes filled with tears. Then she looked up again. "I don't know how to answer you, my dearest daughter. That is why I wanted you here as soon as possible. Before word spreads."

"Then you shouldn't have sent me away yesterday to teach your littlest daughter to hunt," Hippolyta answered her bitterly. "It's already too late to stop this news from reaching your people."

Just then the door to the bedchamber flew open, and a dozen warriors filed in, led by the hawk-faced Valasca. They were in full armor, shields, and helmets, and the noise they made marching into the chamber was deafening.

Valasca's bronze helmet cast deep shadows over her face, emphasizing the sharpness of her cheekbones and nose. A Gorgon's head decorated her shield. She looked as fierce as any goddess.

The infant started crying, a thin, high-pitched wail.

Hippolyta felt something cold settle in her stomach. But when she saw her sister Orithya in the second row of the troop of warriors, as well as a smirking Molpadia standing in the back of the group, her cheeks got hot with anger.

Halting at the bed foot, the battle queen slowly removed her helmet. Her black hair was caught up in a warrior's knot. She stared down at the naked infant. "A boy," she said, making it sound like a sentence of death. Which it was.

Looking accusingly at Demonassa, Valasca let her right hand rest lightly on the double-headed ax that hung from her belt. It was a threat, and it worked. Old Demonassa stepped back but did not lower her eyes.

"Did the omens give no warnings?" Valasca said in a cool voice.

The old woman shrugged. "The omens were obscure."

As usual, thought Hippolyta.

"I thought you had more magic than that," Valasca said.

"I saved my magic to ease the birth and deliver the child safely," the old woman answered.

"You needn't have bothered," Valasca said.

On the bed Otrere drew the baby closer to her breast. "What the Fates decide cannot be undone."

"No, Otrere, you mistake it. This is quite easily undone," Valasca answered in her cold voice. "A cloth over the child's face. A knife across its throat. You know the laws, Otrere, and they bind our queens even more than they bind the rest of our race."

Otrere bent her head, but whether in obeisance to her fellow queen or to look at the child again, Hippolyta couldn't have said.

"A queen," Valasca continued, her voice filling the room, "may bear only one live son. If the second grows up, he will bring about the destruction of our race. I know it, you know it. By the goddess, we *all* know it. Let this child live, and we break the pact made with Artemis by all the mothers before us. The goddess has not protected us all these years so we can be destroyed by one boy child!"

Otrere didn't answer, but a single tear escaped her right eye. Hippolyta longed to wipe it away before it shamed them all.

"You and the priestess did not take the easier way, so now you must sacrifice this child with your own knife upon the altar of Artemis," Valasca said. "Such is our law. The goddess has willed it."

"I cannot." Otrere's voice was low but adamant.

"Then you must give up your throne, and another will perform the sacrifice," Valasca said. "Either way, Otrere, the boy dies."

Otrere looked up, her eyes now clear of tears. "We all must die, Valasca. But this child is innocent of any wrongdoing. Only I, who desired one last child before I could have no more, am to blame." She sat up straighter and looked slowly around the room as if addressing every woman there. "The child can be returned to his father. Like his brother before him. If anyone is to be sacrificed, let it be me."

"Mother, no!" Melanippe and Antiope cried out together.

Hippolyta found she couldn't speak. It was as if a spell of silence had been placed upon her tongue.

Valasca shook her head. "You know that can't be, Otrere. The pact says that the babe is to be sacrificed, not the mother. Killing you—much as I might enjoy it—will not save us from the goddess's will." She signaled two of her older warriors. "Take the boy."

Otrere enveloped the baby in her arms and turned away.

Suddenly, without thinking, Hippolyta found herself moving forward and blocking the two warriors before they could reach the bed. She held her hunting knife chest high, ready to strike.

"Otrere is still your queen," she told them sharply. "Not Valasca, who rules only in times of war. You will not lay hands on Otrere."

"Step aside, Hippolyta," warned a familiar voice.

Hippolyta looked toward the speaker and saw that Molpadia had drawn her bow and it was aimed right at her heart. At this distance Molpadia could not possibly miss.

All at once the baby started to cry again, a thin, mewling sound.

Hippolyta could see her older sister, Orithya, behind Molpadia, looking helplessly from one queen to the other, torn between the oath that bound her to Valasca and the blood that bound her to Otrere. Shaking her head, Orithya suddenly strode forward and shoved the point of Molpadia's arrow aside.

"Do you plan to defile the royal bedchamber with blood?" she demanded, voice shaking. "How is that the will of the gods?"

"The will of the gods is that we obey our own laws." Valasca gave the answer in her stone voice, never taking her eyes from Otrere. "And we will spill blood, even here, to obey them."

"There'll be no killing in this place," Demonassa declared, stepping forward to stand by Hippolyta's side. "That would surely anger Artemis more than anything." At her voice, everyone but Queen Otrere looked at her. "But the child's sacrifice can only be accomplished when the moon is half in shadow, half in light, poised between life and death. And that will not be for ten days yet. Surely you know that, Valasca, who knows the rules so well."

Valasca's face grew even sharper, if that were possible. She looked, Hippolyta thought, quite a bit like her own ax.

"I will take the child and keep him quiet," Demonassa said, adding, "You will want him alive on the altar, or the sacrifice will be worth nothing."

Otrere gave up the child readily enough to the old priestess.

Valasca said softly, "By your own wish you are queen no longer. Another will perform the sacrifice. You will remain here for the ten days with only a single attendant to care for you. After that, you shall be brought for judgment before the court of the Nines."

Demonassa wrapped the child lightly in soft deerskin and walked out of the room, accompanied by Valasca and her guards.

Hippolyta and her sisters followed reluctantly behind, but Hippolyta was thinking: *That gives us ten days, thanks to Demonassa.*

But then she quickly wondered: *Ten days to do what?*

CHAPTER THREE

THE PRISONER

Because her mother was no longer queen, Hippolyta had to leave the palace where she'd lived all her life and move into the warriors' communal barracks. It was more a jolt to her heart than her body. After all, none of the Amazons led pampered lives. Even the queens were trained as hunters and farmers.

Hippolyta had looked forward to joining the ranks of the warriors in two years, when she entered her fifteenth year and had gone on her Long Mission, trekking into the wilderness for a month on her own. Now she was there sooner than anyone had planned.

Being escorted by armed guards to the barracks like a prisoner, being forcibly separated from her younger sisters, made Hippolyta furious. After all, even if their mother had broken a law, *they* had done nothing wrong. But Valasca had insisted that they be guarded in case they tried to do something foolish. Like help their mother escape.

"At least," Hippolyta pleaded with two of the warriors set over her as guards, "let me see how Antiope and Melanippe are doing."

"They are Amazons," said one frostily.

"They will be fine," the other added, though she at least smiled down at Hippolyta.

"*They* are little girls," Hippolyta answered angrily. "And if they have to be apart from their mother, at least—"

"Antiope and Melanippe are in the Halls of Athena," the frosty guard replied, "dwelling along with other girls whose mothers have died, in sickness or in battle."

"Our mother hasn't died," Hippolyta said through gritted teeth.

"Not yet" came the icy reply.

Hippolyta drew in a sharp breath.

The other guard put her hand on Hippolyta's and said softly, "I'll see what I can do."

It took five days before Hippolyta was allowed a short visit with her sisters, accompanied by two guards.

The Halls of Athena was really one large lodge with two wings sitting atop a rise. The girls lived in the smaller wing, in separate rooms.

Hippolyta visited with Melanippe first and found that she'd adjusted well to her new surroundings.

"Antiope does nothing but cry," Melanippe said. "I can't seem to help her. The other girls are mean to us, of course. But they take their lead from the matrons here, who say that Mother intended the Amazon race to die." She looked grim. "It's not true, is it?"

"Of course it's not true. Mother doesn't want anyone to die. Not even the baby."

"I *knew* it!" Melanippe said. Relief suffused her face.

"Be strong." Hippolyta gave her sister a quick hug, stood, and went across the hallway to Antiope's room.

Antiope was sitting all alone on a narrow bed, staring out the window and across the top of the palisade to where the black waters of the Euxine Sea lay along the horizon.

"Antiope?" Hippolyta called, but the little girl didn't seem to hear. *"Antiope."*

This time Antiope turned and stared at Hippolyta, tears coursing down her cheeks.

In two long steps Hippolyta was across the room and onto the bed, wrapping her arms around her little sister. "There, there," she said, sounding exactly like their mother.

"What—" Antiope gulped, started again. "What's the baby done that's so wrong?" She swiped at her brimming eyes with the backs of her hands.

"It's not that he's done anything wrong," Hippolyta whispered into her sister's hair. "It's just that he's a male, and it's our law."

"I hate our law then," Antiope cried. "I wish somebody would take it away and burn it!"

Trying not to smile, Hippolyta sat back and looked into Antiope's dark eyes. "Without laws, sister, there would be no Themiscyra. No Long Mission. No—"

"Then I guess I don't hate *all* of it," Antiope said. She bit her lower lip. "Just the dead baby part."

Hippolyta nodded. "I hate that part too. But it *is* the law." Then she embraced her sister again, stood, and was gone.

The next day Hippolyta heard that Otrere had been moved from the palace into the prison by the palisade where criminals were commonly kept. The rumor was that Valasca was trying to starve her into submission.

Or just starve her, Hippolyta thought. *Then Valasca could proclaim herself queen of both war and peace.* She wondered which lawbreaking was worse, her mother's or the warrior queen's.

For several days Hippolyta attempted to visit her mother. She argued with the two guards at the barracks about it until she wore them down. But the prison guards were of sterner stuff. They turned her back roughly, as if they'd no idea who she was.

"Orders are that no one gets in to see the old queen," they said.

"You can't treat me this way," Hippolyta yelled at them. "I'm her daughter!"

They laughed.

"She prefers sons," said one.

It was the laughter, not the rough handling, that hurt. Hippolyta stormed off toward the drill field, her two barracks guards in tow. They watched as she crossed the field to face her older sister, who was working out with her sword.

"Have you heard what's happening to Mother?" Hippolyta demanded, grabbing Orithya by the sword arm. "She's locked up as a prisoner."

Orithya shook Hippolyta off and wiped her sweaty face with the back of her arm. Her copper hair was braided tightly behind her, but there were little sweaty wisps around her temples. "Otrere brought it on herself by her own stubbornness."

"How can you be so hard-hearted? She's our *mother*!" Hippolyta hated the whine she could hear rising in her voice, like a child wangling for something sweet.

"My heart is no harder than yours," Orithya answered, lifting the sword and once again starting the ritual passes. "But at least I'm realistic. Think, Hippolyta, think. Even if we could change her mind, we wouldn't be allowed in to talk with her. No one is. Especially not the women who agree with her."

"There are some who agree?"

"Of course," Orithya said, punctuating her statements with the sword. "Women who have borne sons themselves. Women with new infants. Women who are merchants and have spent time beyond our walls trading with other tribes. They understand at least, even if they do not agree entirely. But we warriors are upholding the law. No one gets in to see Otrere. No one."

"And whose ruling is that?" Hippolyta asked, though she already guessed.

"Valasca's."

"Of course."

Orithya had gone through the first set of passes— "The Guardian"—and was starting on the second—"The Death Watch." She turned a quarter, then a half, her back to Hippolyta.

"And once the child is dead," Hippolyta said, "what's to happen to Mother then?"

Orithya shrugged but didn't slow her movements. "I don't think there's any provision in the laws to execute a queen. I expect she'll be exiled into the world of men."

"No!" Hippolyta cried just as Orithya turned and faced her, bringing the sword straight down and stopping it abruptly at Hippolyta's shoulder. "How could she survive?"

"She could become one of their slaves," Orithya said. "Or one of their *wives*, which is just as bad." Her voice was as sharp as her sword, but there was a hint of pain in it nonetheless. She lowered the weapon so that it was tip down.

"What are you two *princesses* talking about?" intruded a voice.

Hippolyta turned. The speaker was Molpadia, her bow held loosely in her left hand. She was too far away to have heard any of their conversation.

"We're discussing tactics," Hippolyta answered sharply. "How to set an ambush for a she-cat."

Orithya could not repress a wry grin. "So you'd better be careful, Molpadia."

Molpadia reddened. "You'd both do well to be less haughty now that you're only common clay like the rest of us." Then she glared at Hippolyta, adding, "And *you'd* better plan how to slay your first man instead of mourning our ex-queen."

She turned and sauntered off.

Hippolyta made a face at her back.

"She's right, you know," Orithya said, sheathing her sword.

"She's a sow," Hippolyta answered.

"Perhaps, but she's a brave fighter nonetheless, and we're going to need her when Valasca marches against the Phrygians." Orithya rolled her shoulders and stretched her arms out.

"The Phrygians! I thought Mother made peace with them," Hippolyta said. She suddenly wondered if the baby's being a boy had given Valasca an excuse to do

ward roll on the ground and came up on the far side of the men, holding the ax in both hands.

"You fool, Phraxos," Dares said. He motioned to his men, who, without a word, widely flanked her on both sides till she was inside a large circle with the baby on the outside.

Hippolyta's mouth went dry as a sun-baked rock. She could feel the blood pounding at her temples. Molpadia had taunted her about slaying her first man. How Molpadia would laugh now.

"Give me the child," she heard her own voice say, as if it were coming from somewhere far away. "And let me be on my way."

"Amazon or not, girl, you're no match for six Trojan warriors. Put down your weapon before we have to hurt you," Dares said. He held out his left hand to her, but the right hand held his sword at the ready.

"Trojans!" Hippolyta exclaimed. "But that's where I'm headed. I'm going to Troy to see King Laomedon."

The men began to laugh, a sound like growing thunder, but Dares silenced them with a raised hand. "And why must you see the king?" he asked.

"I have a message for him from Otrere, queen of the Amazons," Hippolyta said. "I'm her daughter, Hippolyta, Amazon princess."

At that the laughter became a cloudburst, and the sound of it made the baby cry.

"Surrender your weapon," Dares said, "and I promise to speak to the king for you."

"What proof do I have that you'll do what you promise?" Hippolyta asked.

"Only my word as a Trojan." He smiled, holding out his hand once again.

"Only your word as a *man*," she said, her voice full of scorn.

"That will have to do," Dares answered.

Hippolyta thought quickly. "Swear by your gods."

"Captain," said Phraxos, "let's just take her."

Nyctos grunted his agreement.

Dares held up his hand. "I swear by my gods that I'll speak to the king for you. You'll be our guest in Troy. Now give me the ax."

Knowing that she had gotten as much out of the man as she could, Hippolyta said, "And I swear by Artemis that if you're false, I *will* kill you."

The men began their thunderous laughs again. But again Dares stopped them. "Done, young Amazon princess. The ax?"

She gave him the ax, handle first, and the bow. They let her keep the arrows, which they considered useless by themselves. She smiled to herself. They hadn't seen how she'd used one on Molpadia.

Dares handed back the baby, and Hippolyta fed him the last of the milk. They let her milk the goat, then set it free. The horrid creature caprioled over the nearest hill and was gone, not even looking back once.

As she tied little Podarces on her back once again, she thought: *Stupid goat. I saved you from the wolves, and you run right back to them.*

Then Nyctos boosted her up onto the little mare, but Dares held the reins so that she couldn't even think about escaping.

And so, led by the Trojans, Hippolyta rode out of the small rounded hills and down into the city itself.

CHAPTER EIGHT

ON TO TROY

Troy.

She'd expected Troy to be much like Themiscyra, perhaps a little larger, but nothing like this. Even her mother's brief description of stone walls hadn't prepared her. The walls were built of huge stone blocks, each the height and length of a tall man.

How had the Trojans managed to move them? she wondered. *Surely only a giant or a Titan could have budged such a colossal weight.*

The city didn't consist of the wooden lodges and single-story buildings she was used to. Rather the stone dwellings and palaces of the Trojans rose twenty and thirty feet above the ground, overtopping even the mighty walls.

She gaped at the sight, and once more the men began to laugh at her.

Riding by her right side, Lyksos said unpleasantly, "I suppose you Amazons live in holes in the ground."

She snapped: "A real warrior would not need such high walls to hide behind." But her heart was not really in her reply.

"We have many enemies," Dares said evenly. "It is their number that decides the height of our walls."

Hippolyta continued to stare at the stones, measuring them with her eyes.

"Gaze well upon these walls, little princess, and think what sort of man must have built them," Dares said. "That man is our king. Laomedon. Do you still want me to keep my promise?"

Hippolyta took a moment before answering, then said, "I *must* see him."

They rode closer, and soon to the west of the walls they could see a blue sea sparkling in the noonday sun. Hippolyta put her hand up to shade her eyes and stared. Half a dozen ships were beached on the sand, their masts dismantled, their sails laid out to dry. As she watched, men busily loaded sacks and jars from the ships onto wagons. Overhead a single black-and-white tern flew by.

"The Aegean Sea, princess," Dares said. "Across those waves pirates sail, seeking plunder and slaves. Our walls keep *them* out as well."

Hippolyta shuddered. Amazons never entrusted themselves to the sea.

They fell behind the convoy of wagons and followed them through the main gate. Seven guards saluted Dares as they passed.

"Hail, Captain," one called. "Good hunting?"

Inside Troy the people were as strange as the houses. Hippolyta saw men and women the color of sand, of earth, of tree bark, of mustard flower. She heard the oddest accents as the merchants loudly traded in the street: silks from Colchis, spices from Egypt, elaborate pottery from Crete.

On her back the baby laughed and cooed, waving his little arm at the banners and bangles. She laughed with him. Even if she was more prisoner than guest, Troy was quite a sight.

Soon Hippolyta became aware that she was not the only one staring. She was drawing some curious looks herself. Sitting straighter in the saddle, she turned her head slightly to whisper back to the baby, "Be quiet. You're the child of an Amazon queen. You're the king's child." But it did not stop little Podarces from his cooing appreciation.

They passed by a marble temple, high and magnificent. Hippolyta looked for signs of which gods ruled here. Over the lintel was the face of a woman in a warrior's helmet. Hippolyta drew in a quick, audible breath.

Dares saw her staring. "Pallas Athena," he said. "Inside the temple is a statue of the goddess." He smiled. "As long as the statue remains, Troy can never fall."

"You place your safety in a woman's hands," Hippolyta said thoughtfully. *Then surely their king will give me what I want in exchange for his son. Weapons and warriors to free my mother.*

"Our king knows how to use the gods to his advantage," Dares said with surprising bitterness.

"No one *uses* the gods," Hippolyta replied.

Dares didn't answer, but his lips were like a dagger's slash across his face.

The royal palace now lay directly before them. Compared with it, the Amazon palace was indeed little more than a hole in the ground.

The palace rose up three full stories. Garlands of flowers decorated the windows; painted shields were affixed to the walls.

"To celebrate our victories," Lyksos pointed out, grinning and showing his bad teeth.

On one side of the courtyard Hippolyta saw a team of four enormous horses being unhitched from a golden chariot.

"The king has returned from his morning ride, I see," said Dares. "That'll put him in a good mood. Lucky for you, little princess."

Hippolyta unstrapped the baby from her back and

handed him down to Dares. Then she dismounted. Turning, she saw the captain staring deeply into the child's face. She saw that he'd figured out exactly why she was here.

Without a word, Dares handed the child back to her. Then he gave his shield and helmet to Nyctos, saying, "I'll see all of you for sword practice before the sun is half down."

Hippolyta stared into the baby's face, as Dares had done. Podarces looked exactly like Antiope at that age. In fact the baby looked like all of Hippolyta's sisters: coppery hair and brown eyes. *Only I am different*, Hippolyta thought, *being black-haired and blue-eyed.* She'd never wondered about that before.

When she glanced around for Dares, he was already halfway up the steps to the entrance to the palace. He beckoned Hippolyta to follow.

She caught up with him, and they passed a line of pillars painted with lifelike eagles and serpents. Then they went through a wide doorway into an entrance hall. It too was painted, only the subjects of these walls were hunting and war.

In the entrance hall stood many men. Courtiers, she supposed, for they looked at ease and were all dressed alike, in graceful tunics with pleated skirts and high-laced sandals. *Certainly not the garb of warriors.*

Dares acknowledged their greetings with a curt nod and led Hippolyta on into the main body of the palace.

They walked along a gallery lined with statues: men wrestling, throwing javelins, fighting with short swords. Hippolyta tried not to stare.

Suddenly a boy came skipping around the corner. He was about nine years old, with russet hair and bright amber eyes. Eating a pomegranate and humming to himself, he was so lost in his own thoughts he almost collided with Hippolyta. She jerked aside to avoid the collision and almost lost her hold on the baby.

"Curse you!" she cried.

The boy pulled up short, swallowed a mouthful of fruit, and glared at her from heavy-lidded eyes. Then he noticed Dares.

"You're back!" he cried.

Dares bowed, little more than a head bob really.

"Did you fight any battles?"

"No battles, Prince Tithonus," Dares replied. "I think the Lydians are keeping to their side of the border after the ambush we caught them in last week."

"Like you," Hippolyta said, still angry at the boy, "the Lydians need to watch where they're going."

The boy turned to her, and this time he stared without any disguise. "Are you a barbarian?"

"An Amazon, my prince," Dares said quickly.

The boy wrinkled his nose and announced loudly, "She's dirty. Someone should give her a bath."

"And someone should teach you manners," Hippolyta said.

Dares gave her a warning frown, but the boy wasn't at all put off.

"Do your men let you talk like that?" he asked. "I thought barbarians beat their women and kept them in cages."

"We have no men," Hippolyta answered, "and no need of them, either."

"You're very savage for a girl." He considered her carefully. "Better not talk to my father that way."

"I will if he talks to me the way you do," Hippolyta declared. The baby in her arms began to fuss, for the sound of argument frightened him.

"Calm yourself, girl," Dares advised. "For the baby's sake, if not your own."

Hippolyta shrugged him off and walked down the hall. Dares followed after her.

"How can you bow and scrape to that spoiled brat?" Hippolyta asked.

"He's a prince," said Dares. "You'd best remember that."

"Well, *I'm* a princess," she replied. "You'd best remember *that.*"

"She's going to get in trouble, isn't she?" Tithonus called, running after them. "I'd like to see that."

Dares turned. "Prince Tithonus, please return to your quarters." His voice was low and respectful, but there was no arguing with it. "Your father will want to see this girl alone."

The boy raised his eyebrows. "Will he? I wouldn't. She smells."

"I *don't* smell," Hippolyta protested.

"She smells no more than any of us who've been out for days sleeping rough," Dares said, keeping himself between the two. "And less than most." He gave the boy a gentle pat on the shoulder to speed him on his way.

The prince kept glancing back as he walked away, but Dares let out a sigh of relief when the boy was finally out of sight.

Around the next corner was a pair of great doors guarded by two men carrying long and cruel-looking spears. They glowered at Hippolyta but gave way at Dares' command, turning to push open the heavy wooden doors.

This room was even more elegant than the rest. The ceiling seemed supported by the slenderest of carved pillars. A series of mosaic tiles, arranged in patterns, made up the floor.

In the center of the room was a pool of bright blue water. There two pretty young women in delicate silken robes were dabbling their feet.

On the far side of the pool a man as golden and maned as a lion reclined on a couch. He looked up languidly, like a great beast roused from sleep, his gaze settling on Hippolyta.

"Prisoner of war, Dares?" He sounded both self-assured and amused.

"No, my king," Dares answered, keeping his eyes firmly lowered.

The king looked searchingly at Hippolyta and the baby. Then he said, "People usually bow when they come before me." He said it softly, but even to Hippolyta it sounded like a threat.

"I am a princess of the Amazons. I bow before no man," she replied.

The king's head went back, and he roared with laughter. When he laughed, the rough planes of his face resolved into something resembling beauty.

Then he stopped laughing as suddenly as he'd begun and looked at Hippolyta again, his eyes narrowing. "I know what you are, little Amazon. I have seen many of your sisters. Even loved a few. What I don't know is why you've brought your little bundle here."

He stood and walked over to Hippolyta. He was tall and wide-shouldered. His golden beard poured down his chest like a glittering wave. His long white robe was trimmed in purple and cinched in by a silver belt studded with red and green stones.

In spite of herself, Hippolyta was impressed. *Surely Zeus himself looks no more kingly*.

"She's here because of the baby," Dares said.

The king leaned over and looked at the child, who reached out for his beard. "Why should this child concern me?"

"I must speak privately with you, King of Troy,"

Hippolyta said. "My mother, Otrere, commands it of me."

At her mother's name, King Laomedon looked up, for a moment startled. Then he snapped his fingers to summon one of the girls.

"Take the child, Artemesia. Treat it well till I ask for it again," he commanded.

"It's a boy," Hippolyta said, handing the baby to the girl. "His name is Podarces." *Strange*, she thought, *how reluctant I am to give up this little burden now.*

"All of you but this little barbarian leave me," commanded Laomedon.

"Your Majesty, are you certain—" Dares began.

Hippolyta wondered whether he wanted to stay for her protection—or the king's. She was about to say she could handle herself when Laomedon interrupted.

"Check the defenses on the north wall, Dares." He waved his hand. "I need no help from you here."

Dares bowed low and, with a final warning glance at Hippolyta, left the chamber.

CHAPTER NINE

KING LAOMEDON

he king walked over to a table and poured himself a cup of wine. He did it with deliberate slowness, like a great beast deciding its next move.

When at last he looked up, he asked, "What is your name, daughter of Otrere?"

"Hippolyta," she answered. "Princess of the Amazons."

"But not the oldest of Otrere's brats," he said.

"Second oldest," she admitted.

He didn't say anything for a long moment but drained the cup of wine halfway. Hippolyta felt every bit of the time stretching out, like a leash around her neck.

"Otrere," Laomedon mused. "Lovely copper hair. Amber eyes. Nice smile. We spent some time together. Twice." He grinned, and the wine glistened on his lips.

Hippolyta hated the way he spoke of her mother, as if she were a broodmare he'd owned.

"We last met some months ago, on the Phrygian border by Aphrodite's grotto." The smile grew broader as he remembered. "I asked her to stay longer, for she matches me in spirit. I like that. But she would not. You Amazons are a restless lot." Now the smile was incandescent, like a candle before it burns down a house. "Take her my warmest regards when you go."

"She needs more than your"—Hippolyta spit out the next two words as if they were some filth in her mouth—"warmest regards." Drawing in a deep breath, she said, "She needs more because of that child of yours."

"The child you brought?"

He's toying with me, Hippolyta thought. *He knows very well the child is his.* But she couldn't think why he should be doing so.

"Yes," she said, "your son. Do you deny that he is yours, King Laomedon?"

He shrugged, finished the wine, and set the cup back on the table. "I saw a resemblance to her. Not to me. Still, she has no reason to lie about such a thing. So, you've brought him to his father's house, as is your custom. Very well, princess, you've done your duty. If you go to the kitchens, they will feed you before you leave."

He reached across the table to a bowl of grapes and plucked several, ready to pop them into his mouth.

Hippolyta walked over and almost put her hand on his arm, before thinking better of it. "My mother needs your help," she pressed. "The mother of your son, Podarces, needs your help."

He paused, a grape halfway to his lips. "*My* help? Amazons never ask for help from men. They just use them to beget children and leave." There was an undertone of anger in his voice, as if some anger with Otrere's refusal to stay with him lingered.

"Because Mother wouldn't sacrifice the boy on Artemis' altar but sent him here instead, she's been cast in prison," Hippolyta told him.

This time the king looked at her with great interest. "But when she sent me Tithonus, there was no such trouble," he said.

Tithonus! That little . . . brat? The other brother? Hippolyta could not believe it. But she had to answer quickly and not show her surprise.

"It's against our laws for a queen to bear more than one live son," Hippolyta said, her voice barely a whisper. She would not tell him why.

A mocking smile lit Laomedon's handsome face and changed it horribly. "Now we come to it! You Amazons thrive on superstitions, like crows feeding on dead flesh. Ha!"

Why, he's just as brutish and selfish as any man, only

with a prettier face. Oh, Mother, how could you have let that face seduce you? Hippolyta thought. But then she realized she was being unfair. Her mother had sought out a king to her queen, power to her power, beauty to her beauty. Her only interest had been to bring forth a strong, handsome child. She had not expected a boy.

But Laomedon was still Hippolyta's only hope. She would have to put aside her disgust for him and beg for her mother's life. "Queen Otrere has been stripped of her throne and will be tried for sacrilege."

He popped a grape in his mouth. For a moment he savored the grape. "It is of no interest to me." He glanced down, savoring the look of astonishment on her face. "And what would you have me do, little princess? Lead an army into Amazon country and set Otrere back on her throne? Leave my own city unguarded, my people unprotected, to march my troops through our enemies and into a barbaric country to settle a quarrel between savage women? Do you think I'm mad?"

"My mother has given you a child," Hippolyta cried. "No, she has given you two children."

"So have many women. I will not go to war for them."

"So she means *nothing* to you?"

Raising an eyebrow, he said with slow deliberateness, "My horse means something to me. When he dies, I will get another. I value my sword, my shield, my guard."

Hippolyta couldn't contain her anger any longer. The man had mocked her, her mother, her people. She lashed out an arm and knocked the bowl of fruit from the table. Grapes flew in all directions.

"You're no king!" Hippolyta raged. "The lowest beggar in the streets has more honor than you."

"Guards!" he thundered. But even before the doors could be flung open, he grabbed her by the hair and threw her to the floor. "*I* am the king, and I will decide what is honorable here in Troy."

She looked up, more surprised than hurt. "May the gods curse you, King Laomedon."

His face darkened. "They already have."

Just then the guards burst in.

Laomedon ran a hand down his tunic, smoothing it. "Take her to the cells."

The guards seized Hippolyta by the arms and yanked her to her feet. She struggled against them, but they were too strong.

"You needn't be gentle," the king said as the men bundled her out of the door. "She's an Amazon, which means she has no tender female sensibilities to injure."

They hauled her out of a back entrance and across a bare yard where soldiers were practicing with their spears. She tried to kick at the men who held her, but they were used to such tactics.

One of the spear handlers yelled out, "Leave her with us for an hour, Caracus, we'll show her how to behave."

But the guards didn't reply, merely dragged her to a large stone building standing on the other side of the courtyard. There they hauled her through a thick wooden gate and on inside.

A stiff-legged jailer led them past a long row of locked cells from which hooting and cursing voices called out.

"Let her go!"

"Bring her here!"

"May your wounds never heal, jailer!"

"The gods look down on your injustice, Laomedon!"

They stopped in front of a heavy wooden door, which the jailer opened with a large bronze key. Then the two soldiers threw her inside.

Stumbling forward, she remembered at the very last minute to tuck in her head and roll. She fetched up against the far wall, humiliated but unhurt. She heard the soldiers laugh uproariously as they slammed the door shut.

Struggling to her feet, Hippolyta felt a twinge in her shoulder, where it had struck the wall. The roots of her hair stung where Laomedon had grabbed her. She must have twisted her ankle slightly when she tumbled into the cell. But what hurt most was her pride.

She limped over to the cell door, glad no one could see her, and looked out of the small grille. She could see neither soldiers nor jailers.

Which doesn't mean there's no one there, she

reminded herself. *Only that I cannot see farther.*

Wrenching herself away from the grille and the light, she began to pace the confines of the cell. It was a much bigger place than the one her mother lay in, back in Themiscyra. But that cell at least had been clean. This one was disgusting. The walls were dank, the floor scattered with a thin layer of dirty straw.

Hippolyta tested the door with its small barred window.

Thick, sturdy, unmovable.

She felt along every inch of the walls.

Even thicker, sturdier.

She sat down on the floor to think. But every thought led back to one: *I have no friends here, no allies. I am at the mercy of a heartless king.*

In the evening—she knew the time only because the jailer told her so—she was given a bowl of thin, cold gruel. An armed guard stood by her as she ate, to prevent any trouble.

"Eat up," sniggered the jailer. "We want meat on you for tomorrow."

She dashed the empty bowl at him, but it missed, and the guard struck her in the chest with the butt of his spear. She fell backward, managing to miss hitting her head on the wall. But she lay there, pretending to be knocked out. That way she could avoid more of a beating, and quite possibly she might hear something to her advantage.

The sniggering jailer said, "Spirited all right."

The guard grunted. "Not that it'll do her any good. She's scarcely a bite as it is."

They left, locking the door behind them, and darkness seeped into the cell.

Scarcely a bite! What did they mean? She'd heard of kingdoms where prisoners were thrown to wild animals. Or maybe Laomedon was that vilest of creatures, one that devoured his own kind.

She shivered and started to whimper. Then she stopped herself. "Amazons do *not* cry," she whispered.

But she was cold, hurt, lonely, scared, and a long way from home.

She didn't cry. But in her sleep, something wet ran down her face from her eyes. She wiped it away without ever waking.

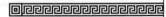
A BROTHERLY VISIT

S he woke from a deep sleep when someone tapped on her door. Flinching back, she rubbed sleep from her eyes. Then curiosity overcame her, and she went to the door.

Standing there was the horrid little prince, Tithonus. "Shh," he said.

She thought: *If I can get him in here, I could take him hostage. Then they'd have to release me and—*

"Shh," he said again, finger to his lips. "Don't wake the others."

Her plans for escape gave way to curiosity. "How did you get in?"

He looked puzzled at her question. "Why, I told the

jailer to let me in. I'm the prince, after all. I said I'd have him thrown in the sea if he didn't do as I commanded."

"Yes, that's exactly what your father would have said," Hippolyta noted sourly. Suddenly she couldn't bear the sight of him. He was just a stupid, boastful, overindulged little boy playing a prank. "Go away," she said sullenly, moving back from the door.

"What?" He seemed genuinely shocked.

"I said—" and she spoke slowly over her shoulder as if talking to a tiny child—"go . . . a . . . way."

There was a pause. Then Tithonus said, "You're really not very nice, are you?"

Hippolyta sighed. "No, I'm not. I'm not nice. I'm a barbarian—remember? And I need my sleep. So go away." She found the small pile of dirty straw that served as her bed and sat down.

"No. I don't want to. I want to ask you a question," the boy said. "About my mother." He no longer sounded so pleased with himself. In fact he sounded as if he were on the edge of pleading. "The queen of the Amazons."

Hippolyta looked up sharply. She could not see his face at the grille. He was too short for that. "How do you know—"

"Father told me. Tonight. I'd always wondered . . ." His voice was now a small boy's, light, uncertain.

Sighing, Hippolyta stood and went back to the door and stared through the grille. For a long moment she looked down at him. In the torchlight, his hair was darker, almost brown. There was a shadowy smudge under one eye.

"Her name is Queen Otrere," she said at last. "She's my mother too."

"Then," he said slowly, "we're family."

She shook her head. "No, we're not. I left my family back in Themiscyra. My mother and sisters. Your family is here."

"But we share—"

"Blood. We share blood. That's all. Now go away. Or get me out of here." There, she'd said it. Without whining or pleading.

"I brought you a pastry," he said. His skinny arm reached up and into the grille. There was a dark circular something in his hand.

Hippolyta hesitated to take anything from a son of Laomedon, but it was too tempting. She snatched the honeyed pastry from his fingers before he had a chance of pulling it away.

"You must be very hungry, sister," he said.

"I've been hungrier," she replied. "And don't call me *sister*!" She ran a finger across her lips to wipe up the rest of the honey, then sucked greedily on the finger like baby Podarces on the wineskin teat.

"Don't bother to thank me," he said, now sullen. The shadows only deepened the pout on his face.

"You came here to ask a favor of me, boy. I've asked you for nothing." Hippolyta drew back a bit from the grille. *Except,* she thought, *to get me out of here or go away. Neither of which he's done.*

"You should thank people when they're kind to you."

She moved forward again and leaned right up against the bars. "Kind would be a soft bed and a clean bath. Kind would be somewhere away from here. I'll thank you when you set me free."

He backed away a step, then moved forward again. "Our father won't allow it."

She shivered. "*Your* father, not mine." But she wondered.

Tithonus was silent.

"Your father doesn't care if our mother lives or dies," Hippolyta said. "I asked him to help her, and he laughed. Then he threw me in here."

"He's—it's . . . hard work being king. He doesn't have time for everybody." Tithonus' face got a pinched, closed look.

Hippolyta laughed. "Ha! Not even time for his son's mother." Then she realized that he had sounded sad, almost apologetic. Suddenly she understood. In a quieter voice she added, "So he's got no time for you, either, eh?"

"That's not true!" Even in the flickering torchlight she could see him flush. His chest was heaving. "Dares— Dares says that things are hard. We're surrounded by enemies and—" He shut his lips together as if he'd admitted too much. "I just wanted to know about *her.* About Queen Otrere."

"What do you want to know?"

The boy leaned forward, whispered eagerly, "What does she look like?"

Hippolyta backed away for a moment, thinking. The father was out of her reach, but not the son. She smiled grimly and went back to the grille. "She's ten feet tall with big purple eyes. She has snakes for hair, and she eats little boys for breakfast!"

Tithonus' lower lip quivered, and he disappeared into the blackness. She could hear him trying to stifle his sobs.

Serves him right, Hippolyta thought. But she felt bad. He'd been such an easy target. And he *had* brought her a pastry.

She called out, "Pssst. Prince. I'm sorry for saying that. Come back tomorrow and bring me two pastries, and I promise I'll tell you what you want to know."

He came back into the light, looking a bit whey-faced. "Tomorrow? But tomorrow will be too late."

She felt a stone in her stomach. "Too late for what?"

"Too late for you," he whispered.

"What do you mean?" The stone in her stomach got heavier.

But he was gone, running off down the corridor as though in fear of his life.

Hippolyta went back to the little pile of straw and sank down onto it. Any impulse to sleep was now gone. She was suddenly and awfully wide awake.

What has Laomedon planned for me? she wondered, remembering the guard's words: "Scarcely a bite." Remembering the king saying that he was cursed. Remembering that she had lashed out at him. At a king. In his own country.

I guess I'm going to find out, she thought miserably. *And soon.*